TRACING

the

CAPE ROMAIN

ARCHIPELAGO

TRACING
the
CAPE ROMAIN
ARCHIPELAGO

BOB RAYNOR

THE
History
PRESS

Published by The History Press
Charleston, SC 29403
www.historypress.net

Images are courtesy of the author unless otherwise noted.

Cover image: A view from high above the marshes of the Cape Romain area. *Courtesy of S.C. Department of Natural Resources, Technology Development Program.*

First published 2009

ISBN 978.1.59629.808.8

Library of Congress Cataloging-in-Publication Data

Raynor, Bob.
Tracing the Cape Romain archipelago / Bob Raynor.
p. cm.
Includes bibliographical references and index.
ISBN 978-1-59629-808-8
1. Romain, Cape (S.C.)--Description and travel. 2. Cape Romain National Wildlife
Refuge (S.C.) 3. Raynor, Bob--Travel--South Carolina--Romain, Cape. 4. Raynor,
Bob--Diaries. 5. Sailing--South Carolina--Romain, Cape. 6. Natural history--South
Carolina--Romain, Cape. 7. Walking--South Carolina--Romain, Cape. 8. Romain,
Cape (S.C.)--History. I. Title.

F277.C4R396 2009
917.57'910444--dc22
2009030534

To Susan, Sara and Eliot

CONTENTS

PREFACE

Between the coastal developments to the north, punctuated by the high-rises of Myrtle Beach, and the suburban beach communities near Charleston to the south, stretches a section of undeveloped and protected coast. Around fifty miles long, the area has a special international status as a UNESCO Biosphere Reserve. Cape Romain and the Santee Delta bulge out into the Atlantic Ocean, defining a wide area of barrier and marsh islands between the beach and the mainland. These islands form a Lowcountry archipelago of islands, surrounded by bays, sounds, creeks and man-made waterways. The protected status of these islands and waters derives from their pristine quality and the diverse and abundant wildlife. Though a majority of the centerpiece of this reserve, Cape Romain National Wildlife Refuge, is a Class I Wilderness Area, man has left his footprint throughout in both subtle and more substantial ways: Native American shell middens, rice fields and their hydrological works, migratory waterfowl impoundments and lighthouses. The combination of natural and cultural history creates an alluring fabric for this archipelago.

The area has fascinated me for some time, and my intensive experiences a few years ago resulted in *Exploring Bull Island: Sailing and Walking Around a South Carolina Sea Island*. It is only natural for me to consider the broader and much larger territories to the north of Bull Island. The distance from the mainland and the difficulty accessing the islands enhance the archipelago's mystique. Viewing the chart of the area, and comparing it with the much shorter travels around Bull Island, is both intimidating and exciting. The more remote places and arduous landings attract me with the promise of adventure and discovery. The potential for close encounters with wildlife exists, along with the possibility of perceiving glimpses of history.

A main means of accessing these new islands and waters is *Kingfisher*, my Sunfish-class sailboat. This vessel has served me well in years of navigating Lowcountry creeks, bays, inlets and the ocean. I imagine encountering shallow areas, oyster banks, strong tidal creeks, narrow waterways and inlets with breaking shoals and landing in places where only kayaks or small johnboats might venture. Like canoes and kayaks, this sailing craft provides for a sensory experience, much heightened by the lack of noise from an engine and for its intimacy with the natural environment. I anticipate challenges: long sails, assaults to *Kingfisher's* rig, adverse conditions, exposure to stormy weather, strain on my body and endurance and limited navigational information. Yet these challenges are an important part of the motivation for these planned voyages. The Sunfish is most efficient when sailed singlehanded, permitting a freedom from concern for others when venturing into often uncomfortable and uncertain conditions. My partnership with *Kingfisher* will take us on new passages to novel places.

These plans include in-depth study and learning. A portion of this educational process will be hands-on, working with biologists whose domain is the archipelago. By contributing some volunteer effort, I will venture out with them on their conservation and management endeavors. Beyond the wildlife management personnel, I want to learn from others who have made their lives in the archipelago.

My mission is to understand the archipelago and interpret to readers, taking them along to access these places. I have a deep appreciation for the existence of this wild territory. Unfortunately, the lands and water are under threat from many directions; significantly, from the intrusion of development along the coast and, in the not too distant future, climate change. Safeguarding this immensely valuable area for all is vital. Individuals must assume accountability for their actions in venturing into the archipelago and be knowledgeable of all regulations. Local residents must be good stewards and accept responsibility for the privilege of living in proximity to these riches.

This archipelago presents an interesting puzzle for those entering its boundaries. I intend to follow the waterways to islands throughout, penetrating into places only allowing the smallest shallow-draft craft. I imagine generating a multidimensional map in my mind of the archipelago and its waters. My firsthand experiences on the water and on the isles will flesh out this map. I plan over several years to venture out to these places, learning as I go and pushing the limits of both *Kingfisher* and me. The voyages will take the reader from one area of the archipelago to another throughout the narrative and will not follow chronology in the telling. Past tales of this archipelago mingled with my current story will illustrate and illuminate these precious places.

ACKNOWLEDGEMENTS

I am indebted to a number of people for assistance with this project. Selden "Bud" Hill, who helped greatly in my first book, again overachieved with his generosity, his sharing of ideas and resources from the Village Museum and his review of the manuscript. William "Billy" Baldwin was also most generous in sharing his extensive knowledge of the area and pointing me in some fascinating directions. Gene Morrison allowed me the rich opportunity to hear about his years on the local waters as a commercial fisherman and about his grandfather, along with answering other queries along the way. Similarly, Bob Baldwin also shared his experience as a local waterman. Other locals filled me in on Jeremy Island through trips to that area: John DuPre, whose family previously owned this island, and my old friend and Nature Conservancy staffer Mike Prevost, who worked on the transfer of the island to Cape Romain National Wildlife Refuge (CRNWR). I was privileged to learn about the lightkeeper of Lighthouse Island, Augustus Wichmann, through an interview with his son, Fred Wichmann.

Sarah Dawsey, wildlife biologist of CRNWR, was immensely helpful in various ways: tolerating my efforts as a volunteer, sharing her extensive history in the loggerhead program and fielding numerous inquiries. Her new boss, Kevin Godsea, provided me with a satellite image of the refuge for assistance in my mapmaking. My friend Gill Guerry, head of graphics for the *Post and Courier* newspaper, helped me greatly in the mapmaking through his considerable expertise, and a young graphic artist in North Carolina, Mason Phillips, mentored me in some of the ways of Adobe Illustrator. Felicia Sanders of the South Carolina Department of Natural Resources took me along on one of her annual nesting surveys on Marsh Island and White Banks and offered other help. Peggy Sloan of the North Carolina Aquarium shared her master's thesis on bottlenose dolphins in the Cape Romain area. Nathan Dias suggested that he could help me find some fine bird photographs through his network, and Chris Snook provided me with wonderful images of a falcon.

Chris Crolley, head of Coastal Expeditions and expert naturalist, has become a good friend throughout this project and insisted on being the person with whom I register my float plans in the event of emergency. I drew on my old friends with publishing expertise, Steve Hoffius and Ted Rosengarten, for their counsel from beginning to end. My fellow adventurer and good friend Rand Schenck gave me a thorough review and criticism of the manuscript and helped make it a better book.

I would also like to thank Laura All and the staff of The History Press for their work in publishing this book and their efforts to find a market in these tough economic times.

Finally, I would like to thank my family. My children, Sara and Eliot, made the commitment to review the manuscript, and their feedback improved the final product. My wife, Susan, was endlessly patient and supportive of my many voyages into the archipelago and countless hours at the computer. She also understands that this project is now over, but another looms.

All of the above help has improved this work significantly; nevertheless, I must take responsibility for any remaining flaws in the text and maps.

NOTES ON MAPS AND NAVIGATION

The creation and provision of detailed maps of the Cape Romain archipelago allow the reader to see the islands and waterways and follow along as if sailing on *Kingfisher*. A main source of information was the Vectorized Shoreline of South Carolina Derived from NOAA-NOS Coastal Survey Maps Developed from 1984–1987 Source Data. While this data provided the main land formations and watercourses, the dated information had some important features in the Cape Romain area wrong. Therefore, a second source was used to correct the most dynamic areas: a digital image derived from color infrared orthophotography of the area accessed from the South Carolina Department of Natural Resources Geographic Information System website. Corrections were made with this data acquired in 2006 to the above South Carolina shoreline.

The resources of the National Oceanic and Atmospheric Administration were also drawn upon for marine forecasts and tide predictions throughout

Legend
for detailed island maps

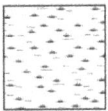

Marsh

Upland

Beach, dunes

- - - ➤

Walks

this project. This information is recorded at the beginning of the story for each trip. The accompanying maps for these trips contain both the sailing courses and the walks on the islands (where applicable).

These maps represent approximations of reality and should not be construed as navigation aids. No soundings are given, and many of the areas that *Kingfisher* penetrated may only be accessed by the most shallow-draft craft possible. Distances, drawn features and directions are estimates only. As I found, published charts are quite limited. Local knowledge will serve as a good guide for those wanting to find their way.

.

PROLOGUE

February 17, 2006

The skies are sunny on this Friday morning at the landing by channel marker #68 along the Intracoastal Waterway. This day is the climax of a warming trend and is enlivened at 10:30 a.m. by a steady southwest wind. I am alone at the landing, and the quietness is etched with the rustling of palmetto fronds and the cries of oystercatchers. The falling tide beckons the launching of the trusty *Kingfisher* for the familiar passage to Bull Island. *Kingfisher* is soon rigged and closehauled, and two tacks put us outward bound in Anderson Creek. A kingfisher on a bamboo stake flies off as we pass on the way to the bay. On the starboard tack and with daggerboard full down, *Kingfisher* is easily accommodated by the high tide on the crossing of Shortcut Shoal into the mouth of Bull Creek. Tacking off and on along the marsh to avoid the outgoing tide, we beat up in the steady light breeze to an easy landing at the public dock on Bull Island. I speak to Wayne Tucker, a U.S. Fish and Wildlife Service staff member, before securing *Kingfisher* and stepping off the dock onto land. The warm southern flow means shorts are in order for this annual celebration of my birthday on the island. Throughout this day, as in many recent moments, my thoughts drift with the southwest breeze toward the north—to the many islands and waterways I plan to explore in the next several years.

After a loop to the Summerhouse dike and past the island cemetery, I peek into the Dominick House and am impressed with the long overdue restoration of this building. Floor sanding is underway, and large bags of pine dust sit on the porch. The newly installed and painted cedar exterior transforms this building from eyesore to attraction. The plan is for several

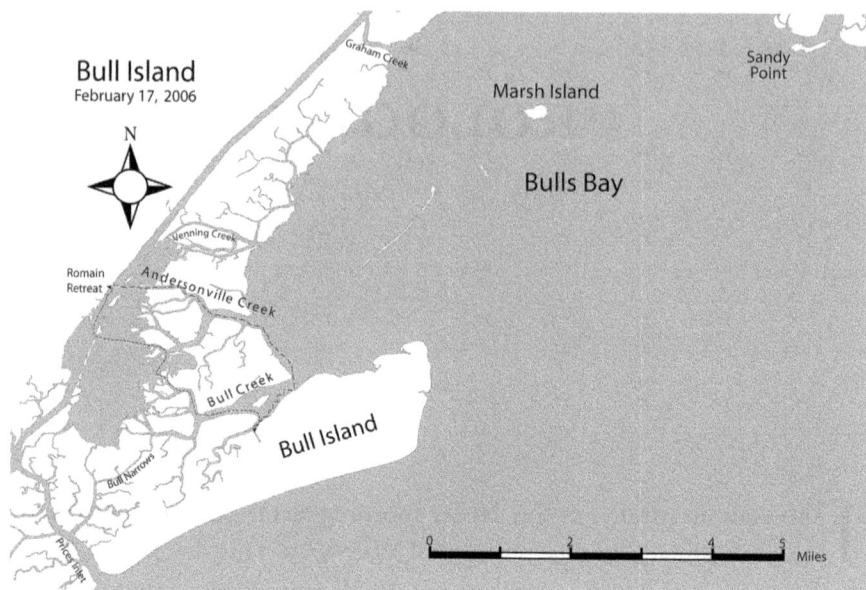

Bull Island
February 17, 2006

N

Graham Creek

Marsh Island

Sandy
Point

Bulls Bay

Venning Creek

Romain
Retreat

Andersonville Creek

Bull Creek

Bull Island

Bull Narrows

Price Inlet

0   1   2   3   4   5
Miles

rooms to be open to the public as an interpretative visitor center. I talk briefly with workers inside, and my alligator agenda comes up. After some gator talk, I head north with my thoughts on the Old Fort Road, cutting through to Sheep Head Ridge Road and then east on Alligator Alley. Alligators small and medium are present; I do not stop long but head for the address of the alpha alligator of Bull Island, now infamously known as "Alligatorzilla," a name penned in a *Post and Courier* news article. Though I have passed his location many times in the past, I only recently learned of his presence. I still must head up Lighthouse Road until I reach the large berm on the left before the next split in the road. Chris Crolley of Coastal Expeditions oriented me to this alligator's lair, and he encouraged me to obtain photos if I am fortunate enough to see him. He recently placed a four-foot stake on the alligator's usual sunning spot as a means to a measurement of this reptile, with estimates of its length ranging between thirteen and twenty feet. I did decline Chris's suggestion that I also take along a tape measure.

I climb a worn path up the steep left side of the berm, and directly across a small pond is a huge alligator, perhaps forty yards away. Yet I am mistaken, for as I look to the right I undoubtedly see Alligatorzilla, of a breathtaking size, virtually unimaginable. The four-foot stake has been pushed over to about a forty-five-degree angle. After several photos with

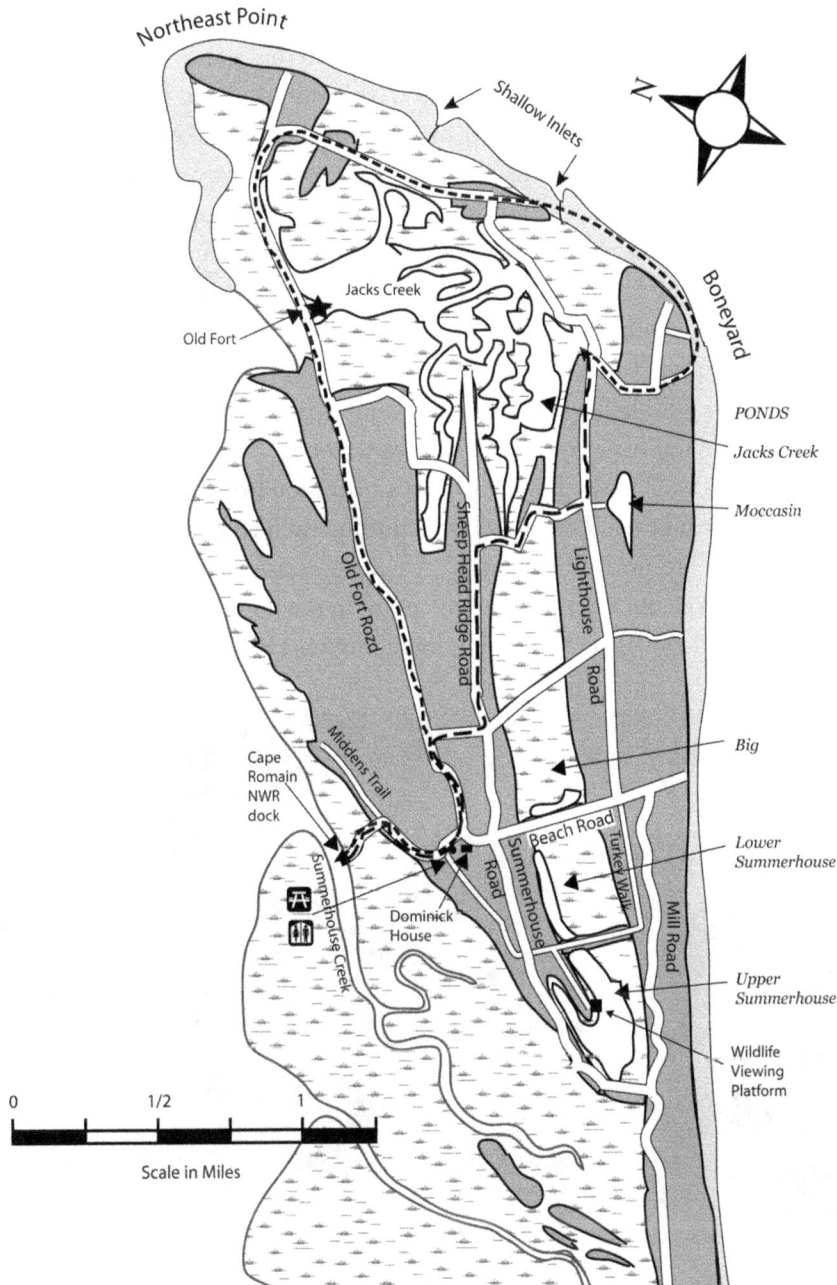

Bull Island
February 17, 2006

Northeast Point

Shallow Inlets

N

Jacks Creek

Old Fort

Boneyard

PONDS

Jacks Creek

Moccasin

Old Fort Rozd

Sheep Head Ridge Road

Lighthouse Road

Big

Cape Romain NWR dock

Middens Trail

Beach Road

Summerhouse Road

Turkey Walk

Lower Summerhouse

Summerhouse Creek

Dominick House

Mill Road

Upper Summerhouse

Wildlife Viewing Platform

0   1/2   1

Scale in Miles

my camera, I consider a closer look. I see that the right side of this finger of Jacks Creek has a small island almost connected to the land where I stand and note that a downed cedar tree has bridged the gap of about ten feet. Selecting a recently cut eight-foot-long wax myrtle stave for both balance and defense, I cross the cedar bridge to the island. I am no longer on a high berm but right next to the dark-colored water. I approach the still unmoving animal. Its slowed metabolism has it soaking up the solar warmth and allowing my distant approach (over thirty yards) for some closer photos. Mission accomplished, I return to the top of the berm to sit for lunch in the warm sun. A coughing spasm brought on by an ill-swallowed bite of sandwich has Alligatorzilla and its neighbor moving and in the water—whether due to feeling threatened or stimulated by the sound of wounded prey, I don't know. But as I recover, I watch this magnificent reptile slowly climb back out of the water with its black and glistening torso, its long tail never quite leaving the water.

It is a short walk to the Boneyard and a transition from one magical world of wildlife to another. The white birds putting on a show with their terrific dives for fish are northern gannets. An eagle cruises by as I pick my way through the skeleton forest around the point to the north, soon encountering the array of deposits on the beach, including cockles, whelks, sand dollars,

"Alligatorzilla," notable bull alligator on Bull Island.

pieces of brick (most likely pieces of the lighthouse foundation) and a fossilized whale vertebrae. But away to the north, and hidden from my vision but assembled in my consciousness, is an archipelago of islands I have just begun to visit. On very clear days on the Northeast Point of Bull Island, I have picked out the low-lying islands stretched out to the east and accented by two lighthouses. The previous month I stood on one of these islands, and from the vantage point of Raccoon Key, I discerned the much higher profile of Bull Island to the south.

After skipping across the shallow inlet, I cross to the Jacks Creek dike, ever closer to the approaching Atlantic, and continue my walk around the impoundment. Arcing around Jacks Creek to the southwest, I observe a raft of white pelicans take off with my approach. Soon past the Old Fort and into the maritime forest, a dead water moccasin, turkey tracks and sightings of fox tail squirrels mark the passage along the road. Seeing Alligatorzilla today is just one of several new discoveries for me in the past year on Bull Island. These finds included a significant shell midden (piles of shells deposited by Native Americans) and a brick cistern of the house of Clarence Magwood on the southern end of the island, shown to me by his son, Andrew. I also made a passage at high tide from Back Creek to Bull Narrows near Price Inlet. Though I have far from exhausted the wonders of Bull Island, I still have my sights set on the islands to the north.

I set sail at 4:15 p.m., about dead low tide, for the sail home via the ferry passage. Men gather oysters on the bank of Bull Creek as I tack up the waterway, making the turns through the creeks in low water. I ignore the navigational rule "red right returning" to explore a substantial creek curving back to the main passage, passing a hunched-over oysterman in waders. In the last section curving to the southwest before the Intracoastal Waterway (ICW), a barge is hard aground. The cargo includes a load of treated lumber and pilings and a large orange excavator brought along to move earth in a major project to change water flow on Bull Island. The unusual vessel doing the pushing is the small trawler *Mermaid Adventure*, hailing from Bennett's Point, South Carolina. A dog on this vessel barks and growls at me as I tack by in the slowly flooding tide. As *Kingfisher* makes the ICW, we bear off. With a gentle wind and increasing following tidal flow, this last short leg of the sail north is simple and barely requires my presence to steer.

On passing, I exchange greetings with some fisherman casting from their boat on the east side of the waterway, and one comments on how peaceful my passage appears. I concur, but shortly the calm is shattered by a resounding *bang!* *Kingfisher*'s bow is the blast's epicenter; I have struck head-on the piling of channel marker #69. Violently jarred from my meditation, I jump up as *Kingfisher* slides to port of the marker. The boom and sail are fixed to the piling as the tide and wind continue to press us tighter. I give a vigorous yank to disengage my boom, sail and sheet from the piling, but the friction both rains exposed barnacles onto the deck and slices the sail near the boom with some resulting peepholes. The need for a window in this old sail is embarrassingly apparent.

So, humbled again on the water, I finish my sail by dragging into the pluff mud at the landing. I am relieved to find no hole in the bow. Repair of the holes in the sail, and completion of a laundry list of other needs for *Kingfisher* and gear, are in order in preparation for a series of voyages to the archipelago of Cape Romain and the Santee Delta. I have made initial trips into these waters to the north already this past year, both on *Kingfisher* and with the U.S. Fish and Wildlife Service loggerhead turtle conservation program. As I plan adventures in the archipelago, I anticipate the experiences waiting to unfold.

RACCOON KEY

Raccoon Key is a sliver of a barrier island, with the majority of the acreage composed of salt marsh. It is bound by the Atlantic Ocean to the south, Five Fathom Creek to the west, Key Creek to the north and Raccoon Creek to the east. Like other islands immediately south and west of the Carolina capes, it is oriented almost east/west, similar to Oak Island (Cape Fear), Shackleford Banks (Cape Lookout) and Ocracoke Island (Cape Hatteras). Unlike these other islands, there is little high ground on Raccoon Key. No maritime forest and virtually no upland exist, merely a narrow strand of beach and sand dunes, though the dunes are even missing in places.

The current Raccoon Key is a shadow of its former self; indeed, the early maps label it "The Raccoon Keys." The former Raccoon Keys were divided by a small tidal creek and stretched from Sandy Point in the west to the current east end of Lighthouse Island. The former island is divided up into four separate islands, with the remains of Sandy Point wearing away rapidly. The extension of Key Inlet creates a deep waterway separating Raccoon Key from Lighthouse Island. Raccoon Creek, a narrower but deep waterway, separates the main section of Raccoon Key from the eastern section. Bob Baldwin, a commercial fisherman working the local waters for years, described to me how much he has observed Raccoon Key eroding away. He noted that the creek entering in the middle of the southern side of the eastern key is really the extension of Raccoon Creek, which curled around about 180 degrees in former times. The location of the former creek bend is now out beyond the surf.

Raccoon Key
May 24, 2006

The eroding of Raccoon Key has been apparent not only to commercial

Raccoon Key

fisherman like Bob Baldwin but also to coastal geologists. Raccoon Key is classified as a transgressive or landward migrating barrier island. Sandy Point was the westernmost end of Raccoon Key and a natural landing. Its erosion and movement landward were certainly accelerated, in part, by a man-made event: the damming of the Santee River and the resultant reduction of sediments supplied to the ocean and nearby barrier islands. A natural disaster, Hurricane Hugo, also had a significant impact on this end of Raccoon Key. The movement toward land was measured in this event as several tens of feet, as observed via the distance traveled by a wash-over terrace across the island's marsh. Seaward from the beach was an exposed layer of backbarrier marsh sediments, along with tidal flat sediments with old oyster beds. The movement was not just toward land but also toward a deep tidal channel, Five Fathom Creek, lying behind the island, and this interaction created a new inlet through Raccoon Key. This inlet is now the access for deep-water craft like shrimp trawlers to reach the ocean. The severed end of Raccoon Key, still known as Sandy Point, which consisted mainly of shell and sediments, has been washing away steadily since Hurricane Hugo and will probably disappear underneath the waters completely (by late 2009, some project).

Raccoon Key was owned by the Lynch family in the eighteenth century. A survey in 1786 for the Lynch estate indicated that the Big and Little Raccoon Keys contained 5,560 acres. Thomas Lynch was an early pioneer and accumulated lands on the North and Santee Rivers that eventually

Raccoon Key
May 24, 2006

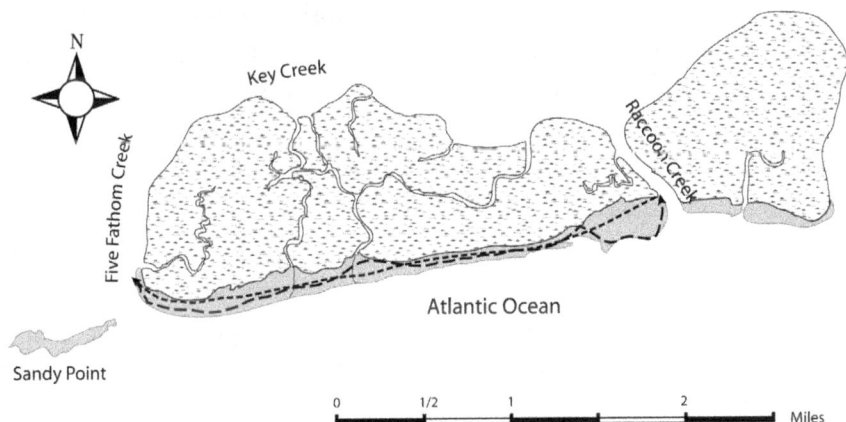

25

became very prosperous rice plantations. Thomas Lynch II, only son of his father, inherited most of the estate, including Raccoon Key. After the deaths of Thomas Lynch II in 1776 and his son (the signer of the Declaration of Independence) in 1779, the properties were divided between Thomas Lynch III's three sisters. Peachtree Plantation went to his sister Sabina, who was married to Scottish native John Bowman. After Bowman's death, his son John inherited his estate, but only after he changed his name to John Bowman Lynch, an action dictated by the conditions of the inheritance. John spent his summers living on a house built on a flatboat that he moved to Raccoon Key.

Forty acres of the east end of the Raccoon Keys were sold to the federal government for the construction of a lighthouse. On a plat dated October 4, 1890, the Raccoon Keys were still intact, without the separation of Lighthouse Island. However, a creek from the backside of the island across the keys marks the place where the division would be made and the opening up of Key Inlet. This plat also declared, "This island was granted in 1788 to Thomas Lynch—now claimed by the State of South Carolina as abandoned."

As with Cape Island just to the north, Raccoon Key has seen its share of shipwrecks. The *South Carolina Gazette* reported on February 17, 1759: "Last Week a loaded coasting Schooner from Santee, belonging to Col. Horry, went ashore upon the Raccoon Keys in a Fog and was lost." In 1815, the British brig *Spring*, captained by Job Colcock Smith, was bound from Liverpool to Wilmington, North Carolina, and was totally lost on the Raccoon Keys. In 1862, the schooner *Chase* of Nassau, running from the United States steamer *Huron*, ran ashore in the middle of Raccoon Keys and was set on fire by her own crew so she would not be captured by the Federal forces.

Historically, Raccoon Key was also a favorite location for loggerhead nesting, only second to Cape Island of the barrier islands along this section of coast. Baldwin and Lofton noted in their study of loggerhead turtles for the United States Biological Survey that Raccoon Key was averaging about two hundred nests per season in 1939. However, with the various changes in configuration of the coast here, Raccoon Key has considerably reduced its size and frontage on the Atlantic Ocean. With Cape Island growing a sand spit several miles to the west, it covered up a portion of Raccoon Key. Much of Raccoon Key's current profile provides little appropriate nesting habitat for loggerheads; they still come, but in greatly reduced numbers. After the western spur of Cape Island broke off in 1996 as the result of Hurricane

Bertha, it has gradually migrated toward and welded onto Lighthouse Island. The loggerhead nests on this section of Cape Island that is now considered part of Lighthouse Island are surveyed and studied as part of the overall loggerhead turtle program in the refuge.

MAY 24, 2006

Low tide 12:35 p.m. Predicted winds SE 10–15 knots; 15 knots in p.m.

We leave Jeremy Creek at 9:10 a.m. in a light wind but a positive outgoing tide. The course is out Five Fathom Creek. Crabbers are working here and there, and farther along, the crew of the blue trawler *Foxy Lady* has anchored and is working on gear. A few tacks are needed to negotiate the turn to the southeast in Five Fathom Creek. Progress is good, and at 10:20 a.m. we reach the end of Raccoon Key, void of other boats. On the other side of the mouth of Five Fathom Creek is a bank covered with a large gathering of pelicans and cormorants.

The proximity of these two species complements their biological association in the bird world order Pelecaniformes. This order includes pelicans, cormorants, darters, gannets, boobies, frigatebirds and tropicbirds. Unlike other birds, Pelecaniformes are totipalmate: their feet have all four toes webbed. No other bird exudes the South Carolina coastal strand more than the brown pelican (*Pelecanus occidentalis*). The pelican family goes back forty million years in the fossil record. They have several characteristics that distinguish them from their cormorant cousins. These include the ability to glide and soar, whether just inches above the ocean surface utilizing the updraft from swells or high in the sky on rising thermals. The very large wings and specialized breast muscles enabling the bird to hold the wings rigid account for this gliding ability. The brown pelican possesses another ability lacking in all the other pelican species: fishing through plunge diving. The huge pouched bill comes into play in its explosive drops into the sea, the height of the drop only exceeded locally by the gannets.

Cormorants are a much more ancient family of birds. The cormorants lack not only some of the advances of the pelican but also their charisma. Cormorants do not have the ability to soar like pelicans and must almost exclusively beat their wings to fly. Since they lack a preening gland, they cannot waterproof their feathers and must awkwardly hold their wings out to dry. The prevalent cormorant in South Carolina and North America is the double-crested cormorant (*Phalacrocorax auritus*). In times past along the coast they were known locally as "niggergeese" and were considered unfit for eating. In modern times, despite their decline from when John James Audubon observed "probably Millions," some people consider them to be a nuisance, much like Canadian geese. Further, they have been labeled fish stealers, taking away from the living of fishermen. Aquaculture managers have fumed about these birds nabbing their pond-grown fish. In some locations, the taking over of islands for nesting colonies by cormorants has crowded out other more esteemed birds. Their growing numbers in the last thirty years have caused an outcry for management, and an average of forty thousand cormorants a year have been killed, along with the oiling of eggs. These birds are common in South Carolina but have not locally become a nuisance.

I make sure that *Kingfisher* is secured to a fixed post on the island, connecting towline, sheet and a piece of blue webbing together for the attachment. My plan is to walk to the east end of the island and back. I grab some gear and head off. This island is noted for its shells, and an abundance of whelks of various sizes sit on the strand. Looking across to the remains of Sandy Point, once connected to this island, the signs of the breach through Raccoon Key are further exposed, with dark marsh sediments showing on both sides of the inlet. The beach curves around the point by the inlet, with no dunes and a minimum of plants. After the curve, some small dunes with increased vegetation exist. Numerous seabirds and shorebirds populate the air and beach: least terns, black skimmers, oystercatchers and brown pelicans. Three trawlers in view are working in the ocean.

At the first of the shallow tidal creeks cutting across the island, the wading is easy, with the water just ankle deep. The shallow water connects with a creek going into the marsh behind the island. The narrowness of this barrier island is striking. Occasionally there is a flight of oystercatchers, and airborne least terns appear to be in nest-protection mode. I meander on my walk, exploring from the low tide line to the dunes and marsh edge. I arrive at the second shallow tidal creek cleaving the beach, also at ankle depth. This creek reaches extensively into the backbarrier marsh.

Beyond this creek, across the beach, there is a narrow marsh with a second sand ridge, sprouting more substantial vegetation, including yuccas.

Raccoon Key

I find an area to cross and explore this sand and shell ridge. I return to the beach and continue to walk east. The lighthouses on Lighthouse Island are appearing closer. The waters of Key Inlet lie ahead, and as low tide is also approaching, there are extensive tidal flats and sandbars extending out from the beach. I take the ridge of the beach extending out into the marsh as far as it will go. Turning down into the cordgrass and heading toward the water, I find firm ground underfoot since the area around this grass is covered with sand.

After wading across several shallow areas, I am out on the extensive tidal flats. Working my way out toward the ocean, there is an interesting sand feature where I must climb a bank about six feet to summit the top of a curving ridge. Water and wind have sculpted the sand into a transient beauty. The tidal flats ahead nearest the inlet are covered with birds. Beyond is the shallow channel where I made my first entrance into Key Inlet from the ocean several weeks before on the sail to Mill Island. Walking around toward the inlet, the view across the water is of the sands of the next barrier island to the east, known currently as Lighthouse Island. Continuing the

Raccoon Key with lighthouses in the distance to the east.

walk, I must wade across some more shallow pools between the higher flats and then make it to the last of the sand flats that transition into marsh at the mouth of Raccoon Creek. This is a good spot to cool off in the water and eat lunch.

I resume the return walk in a more straightforward fashion back to the west. It is already forty-five minutes after low tide, and I anticipate the water will be deeper in the two tidal creeks cutting across the beach. Angling across the sand ridge of one of the tidal flats, I find three beautiful eggs—light green and speckled. I saw these same eggs a week before during the South Carolina Department of Natural Resources (DNR) survey of Marsh Island and White Banks but don't recall the species. I pick a line to walk closer to the water and occasionally slosh through the shallows. The long walk and repeated soaking of my sandals stimulate the development of blisters. The rise of the tide is apparent, and at the first of the tidal creeks the water is deeper but presents a minimal obstacle. I anticipate more of a challenge at the next creek and keep up a brisk pace. Royal terns are in the air, and a pair of black skimmers give their animated call.

Arriving at the second tidal creek, this water is much wider, and the incoming tide is surging in. The crossing will be a challenge, with the tide now having risen one and a half hours from low. I use my hiking stick to probe the depths ahead. As a precaution, I take my digital camera off my belt to hold overhead. In the crossing, the surging water is trying to take me off my feet, and the water comes almost up to my waist. This could potentially be a dangerous place to cross with higher water. Past this obstacle, the last section of the walk is uneventful.

People appear ahead on the beach: three college-age guys fishing in the surf and a woman shelling alone. Two outboards flank *Kingfisher*, and the water level of the inlet has risen to her stern. The other vessel, *Pawleys Girl*, is occupied by a Philadelphia couple, owners of a house on Pawleys Island. Earlier in the day they ran down the ICW from Georgetown. We chat about the fire burning to the north, perhaps on the Santee Coastal Reserve. After raising sail and shoving off, I say goodbye, and soon we are moving well in the strong incoming tide on a reach across the southeast breeze in Five Fathom Creek. Out toward Bulls Bay, a trawler is on the other side of Raccoon Key, heading in. The trawler is coming on when we round the bend into the creek section to the northwest. Sailing on a run, we stay near the starboard bank for the next bend to the northeast.

Raccoon Key

In 1999, the trawler *Lady Lynn*, with captain Chet Anderson at the helm, was heading home after a shrimping trip. A loose line contributed to a man going overboard—the mate, Melvin Garrett. Knowing that Garrett was a non-swimmer, Anderson jumped overboard to his rescue. A recreational boater picked up both men, but Anderson was not breathing. Though CPR was given both on the boat and back on the dock, Anderson died. His death was a catalyst for the creation of the Lowcountry Seaman's Memorial at the Ashley Landing. One of the three stones has a special inscription:

DEDICATED TO
CHET ANDERSON
(1965–1999)
"NO MAN HAS GREATER LOVE THAN HE
WHO LAYS DOWN HIS LIFE FOR A FRIEND.
JOHN 15:13

The trawler astern is in view and closing the distance. We make the point before him, round close to the channel marker and come up on the new course. He rounds soon thereafter and steams by with only one crewman visible on deck. A large crowd of birds—brown pelicans, laughing gulls and royal terns—follows the trawler *Village Lady*. They prepare to get refuse from the trawler's day of shrimping, and more birds are covering the horizontal lines above the trawler's booms. The captain slows to haul up the booms and nets, and as we pass, two men are now on deck. Sailing ahead, we are rapidly passed by a boat coming in from a day of offshore fishing, and the trawler is coming on again. In the narrow stretch of Town Creek, we give the trawler the channel as he passes, and we take off surfing on a couple of waves generated by his passage. We follow his wake into Jeremy Creek.

JEREMY ISLAND

Of the many islands in the Cape Romain National Wildlife Refuge, Jeremy Island stands apart from the others due to its proximity to the mainland. Certainly there are other smaller islands situated next to the ICW, and many of these are the result of dredge spoil deposition. Jeremy owes its uniqueness to the works of man: the cutting of the ICW through here in the early twentieth century, separating this long, narrow upland from its connection to the mainland. It is also the most accessible island in the refuge; after a short boat ride from Jeremy Creek through Clubhouse Creek, one can step onto a sandy beach. This beach is at the beginning of a stretch of waterway called Island Cut, another dug waterway created for the passage of fishing craft to Cape Romain Harbor and the inlet between Cape Inlet and Murphy Island, accessing the ocean. Island Cut seems an appropriate name, since a forested remnant of Jeremy Island exists on the southwest side of the cut. Looking at either an aerial or satellite map of the island and the surrounding area, the connection with the mainland is clear, with Jeremy Island's upland making a visual extension with a peninsula of land to the northeast.

This idea of Jeremy Island as a peninsula separated from the mainland was shared with me by John DuPre. The DuPre family owned Jeremy Island for years, and the island sits across the ICW from the DuPres' mainland property, Palmetto Plantation. John's grandfather sold it during the Depression to a New York family, the Millers. The Millers had property around the world for their outdoor interests. Their travels away from their

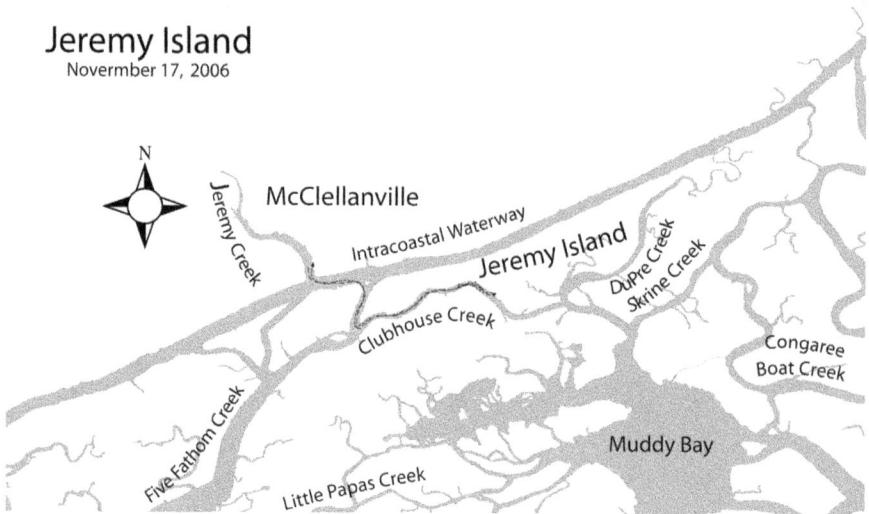

Jeremy Island
Novermber 17, 2006

Manhattan home took them from hunting grouse in Scotland to salmon fishing in Alaska. They purchased this South Carolina property for duck hunting and proceeded to build impoundments for duck marsh on the plantation. Most likely, they also built the duck pond over on Jeremy Island for the same purpose. During this time, John's father, Andrew Hibben DuPre, worked on the property to help manage it. When the Millers became too old for duck hunting, recognizing DuPre's love for this property, they sold it back to the DuPre family.

Jeremy Island was still owned by a collective of John's siblings and cousins at the beginning of the twenty-first century. At this time, no buildings existed on the island. The island and an even larger adjacent marsh island were sizable chunks of private property sitting in Cape Romain National Wildlife Refuge, and the upland of Jeremy provided the potential for future development in this Class I Wilderness Area. A cousin of John at one point attempted to buy out everyone's interests and get control of Jeremy but was unsuccessful due to the many parties involved. When the U.S. Fish and Wildlife Service (USFWS) approached the DuPre family in a bid to buy, they jumped at this opportunity. John stated that this transaction has freed the family from worries of future development right across from Palmetto Plantation.

Jeremy Island

Jeremy Island gets its name from a Native American "king" known as Jeremy. This label is one of the few Native American names retained for islands, creeks and bodies of water in the refuge. The name Jeremy is also still used for the creek penetrating the mainland where the town of McClellanville was initially laid out. The Native American Jeremy was a leader of the Sewee Indians, a group ranging through Christ Church parish. These lands were extensive, and a warrant for five hundred acres of land on the South Santee River obtained by Daniel McGregor at the beginning of the eighteenth century was noted as "formerly of ye plantation of King Jeremy." Jeremy Island itself is the repository of extensive Native American artifacts. Places along the marsh have extensive arrays of these potshards, and sizable middens are scattered around the island. Though the island's Native American heritage has been sampled by residents for years, and studied by a local amateur archaeologist Donald Mackintosh, there has been no professional archaeological survey or study. Mackintosh's collection does reside at the Charleston Museum, packed up and stored for years.

Besides the Native American heritage, Jeremy Island stands out with its maritime forests. Excluding Bull Island to the south, Jeremy is the only other CRNWR island with such extensive maritime forest. Cape and Lighthouse Islands have stands of pines, but Jeremy has a developed maritime forest of live oaks, palmettos, cedars, pines and laurel oaks. Though assaulted by Hurricane Hugo, with signs still visible of many uprooted cedars, some of the sea violence was parried by the extensive marsh fronting to the east.

Jeremy Island
and adjacent islands
November 17, 2006

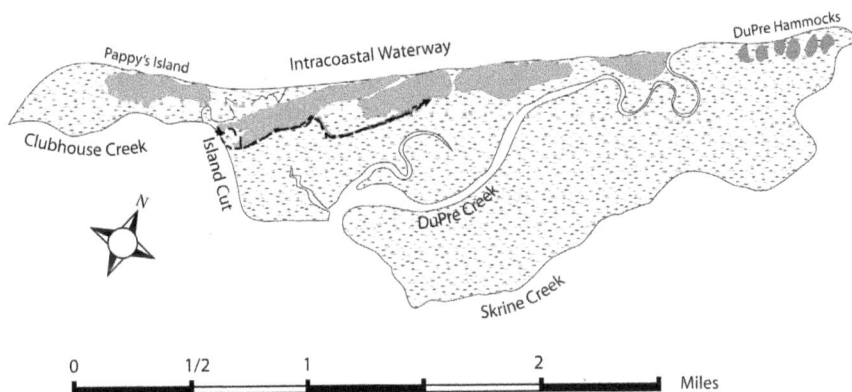

Pappy's Island   Intracoastal Waterway   DuPre Hammocks

Clubhouse Creek   Island Cut   DuPre Creek

N

Skrine Creek

0   1/2   1   2   Miles

The island also has large stands of pines, particularly to the mainland side of the duck pond. The duck pond is no longer a freshwater impoundment but a combination of salt and brackish marsh. Inner parts of the island have other wetland features, and one slough runs across the island from the impoundment to the ICW side. John DuPre mentioned that as a boy he remembers paddling across to the island and then venturing on foot until finding the bateau left in this little creek. From there, he would pole through the wetland until reaching the duck pond.

The sale of Jeremy Island to the USFWS was facilitated by the Nature Conservancy. Mike Prevost, staff member of the Nature Conservancy and a longtime friend, worked directly on that project. On February 10, 2007, Mike and I traveled in his fourteen-foot johnboat for a trip to explore the island.

Mike and I got off before 10:00 a.m. on a beautiful, clear and cool day. In no time, we went through Clubhouse Creek and approached the beach of Jeremy Island. The johnboat was soon tied up to a cedar stump, and we retraced my earlier trip across the marsh finger to the southeast maritime forest and around the point to the eastern marsh. Along this familiar walk on the edge, Mike presented the ecological description of features I have observed: the phases of the marsh. The *Spartina alterniflora* marsh was low low marsh; the other phases were high low, low high and high high marsh. We looked at the vegetation changes in the phases of this distinctive ecotone.

We were not able to cross to the dike around the duck pond due to the water height when we reached the breach, so instead we walked along the upland side of the impoundment. We found solid ground in the old impoundment and walked across it to a high spot populated with little cedars. We had noticed what looked to be a slough through the island on an aerial photo, and we saw a break in the trees ahead. We took this as our path, and as we progressed, another *Spartina* species populated the area closer to fresh water—big cordgrass (*Spartina cynosuroides*). After we continued around the bend in this narrow wetland, we crossed upland through pines. The ground at one point rippled with furrows, perhaps an artifact from Sea Island cotton farming in the past.

Shortly we reached the ICW and, walking north, came across an Army Corps of Engineers geodetic survey marsh. In the past several years I met Doug Springer, a resident of North Carolina who worked on a surveying crew in this area in the 1970s and who probably set this marker. Doug talked about their young crew living in the area, working hard and enjoying the night life. He related that many of the survey markers were nicknamed after young women of their acquaintance.

Mike and I walked to the north end and cut across a gap we had seen on the aerial photo. Getting around to the eastern side, we found the dike, walked for a while and then found a spot to cut across a narrowing ditch. We waded across a section of shallow pond and then across an upland through a stand of narrow pines. After crossing a ditch, we were soon walking through live oaks, palmettos and yuccas. Next, we had to bust through a thicket and found ourselves again in big cordgrass; we thought we were back in the slough. However, the wetland had small open areas with deeper water that Mike felt were gator holes. Treading lightly, we went around these and found higher ground, necessitating more bushwhacking. Finally out into needlerush, we were back in the impoundment. From there, we crossed over to the upland side and retraced our steps along the marsh edge, through the maritime forest and across the marsh finger, back to the beach for lunch.

Departing the beach in Mike's boat, we went east in Island Cut until we reached Dupre Creek and then north and east in this creek between Jeremy Island and the large marsh island to the east. This island of marsh is actually larger in area than Jeremy and its associated marsh. From this perspective, going through Dupre Creek to the east, the duck pond's dike was clearly marked by cedars. The sale of Jeremy Island and the large adjacent marsh island was for $875,000 and included the setting up of a conservation easement on the very northeast end of Jeremy. Part of the monitoring of this easement is an annual observation, and Mike planned to do this today. DuPre Creek narrows dramatically before connecting with the ICW, and I understand why I missed this outlet on a previous trip to Murphy Island. Mike and I took the opportunity to land, with the tide still flooding. We walked across the end and observed that this was clearly dredge spoil. There were cedars and pines, along with other species indicative of dredge spoil islands: hackberry, chinaberry and honeysuckle.

Finding no evidence of previous structures, we cast off again in the boat, heading north. As we passed a tiny hammock in the marsh to the east, we crossed the new boundary of CRNWR. Going farther, we came to six hammocks along the ICW that still belong to members of the DuPre family. Two different parts of the family have kept two and four hammocks respectively. A conservation easement allowed them to keep these hammocks located across the ICW from Palmetto Plantation. The only future building allowed is a four-hundred-square-foot camping structure with a screen enclosure. The USFWS will have the first option on any future sale. We took a quick look at the hammocks from the water for Mike's annual monitoring.

On our return, we decided to look for site #6 marked on the Mackintosh map of Jeremy Island, comparing it with the aerial photo. Making our decision, we landed in an area of cedars. We checked an uprooted tree with what appeared to be potshards, but on closer inspection Mike identified them as echinoderm bodies, a sign of dredge spoil. Walking a little south, we found a possible promising area with live oaks and the feel of a homesite but came up empty. We were looking for foundation remains of a building said to have existed here, the home of Ned Chamberlain. Stewart, the brother of Donald Mackintosh, stated that Chamberlain had lived here and related that this section of Jeremy was known as Chamberlain's Island. But this structure remained hidden from our investigation.

NOVEMBER 17, 2006

Low tide 11:30 a.m. Predicted winds W 10–15 knots.

I am effortlessly sailing out Jeremy Creek at 9:30 a.m. The convenient west wind is making it a breeze heading out. A couple of snowbirds head south, and a few outboards pass in the creek. People are bundled up today; a couple heading out with a Georgetown fishing guide even have face masks on. I entertain the idea of landing first on the hammock to the south of Island Cut, appearing like a small split-off part of Jeremy Island, but the landing appears very muddy. The landing on the sandy beach of Jeremy Island will be easy and quite a luxury compared to my Lighthouse Island trips in the last month. A massive overturned cedar tree above the high tide line on the beach makes a fine mooring.

After changing shoes, I take a look at the large midden closest to the beach. It has signs of excavation by relic hunters. There are readily seen potshards on the beach, and lots of clam shells. The sun is very bright, balancing the cool air. This beach would have been an excellent canoe landing, and the

Jeremy Island

Native American artifacts seem to mark the spot. However, it is unclear what the creek system was like prehistorically, since the Island Cut waterway was made sometime in the early twentieth century. Hopefully, the island's new status as part of Cape Romain National Wildlife Refuge will give some protection to the Native American heritage to be found all over the island. Exploring this heritage will be on the agenda for the walk around the island today, and a map marking some of the middens will be the guide.

I head east along the beach of Island Cut until meeting up with a large finger of marsh jutting into the island's high ground. A tiny creek feeds the marsh with salt water, and I choose to walk along the edge of the marsh, spread out into a big *U*. The edge between the salt marsh and needlerush communities is distinct. The competition between these two botanical communities creates a sharp boundary, referred to as zonation, and makes a decent "path" for my walk. Soon the marsh solidifies into a flat, enabling a crossing to the east side. I step into the dense maritime forest of live oaks, palmettos, laurel oaks, pines and cedars. Wherever an uprooted tree exposes its root ball, shell midden is found. I pick my way through the many Hugo-overturned cedars on a heading out to Island Cut.

Reaching the creek, I walk around the southeastern end of the island, finding a second midden with extensive potshards. After the rounding, my path is on the long axis of the island, walking the edge again between salt marsh and upland in a northeasterly direction. The island is much bigger than I anticipated. I pass the midden on my map marked "4." There is a fine view to the east across extensive marsh and out to Murphy Island in the distance. The slight elevation gradient I cross holds the transition from cordgrass to sea ox-eyes and needlerush. I take peeks occasionally into the island's interior: there is no rush today.

There is an area jutting out ahead from the island, and on my map it is designated "Duck Pond." It has an unusual feature, being rimmed on the outside by trees. Closer inspection reveals that they are cedar trees growing on top of a man-made dike forming the pond on the marsh side. When my path meets up with the diked pond, a small creek cutting through the dike blocks the way. The tide is still falling, and I find a board to span the small creek over to the dike. The dike's edge is walkable, so I continue on. A large stand of prickly-pear has colonized the dike, and obviously the cedars are very happy here, growing to a height of fifteen feet. It is a very sunny day, and I keep my eyes out for alligators on the dike but see none.

More middens are charted on my map outside of the dike. The dike is sizable, and I wonder about its origin. From the dike, the pond appears as a wetland dominated by needlerush with no open water. With the breaching of the dike by the creek I crossed, the impoundment has reverted from fresh water to salt and brackish marsh. A solid wall of pine trees, marking the upland, appears across the wetland. Pine trees also grow on the dike, along with live oaks. After passing one midden, I come to the marked "2" on the map, and it has a large live oak growing on top. This midden hammock is just outside of the dike and is also covered with yuccas. I am close to the end of the pond, as the dike is curving back toward the body of the island. Some open water stands at this end of the impoundment. I must take care and not step on the fiddler crabs sharing the edge with me. The view to the east includes Murphy Island, Cape Island and its stand of pines, matched by the pines of Lighthouse Island dwarfed by the lighthouses. And far off, past these islands over the ocean, tiny clouds make their appearance.

The original plan was to walk around the entire island, but I was not prepared for its length. At the end of the dike, I make my turn and retrace my steps. There is another marked midden at the northeastern end of the island, but I will postpone my visit for another day. Instead, a look at "3" is in order, close to the end where the pond begins to narrow. I pick up dune devil-joints on this site, the long spines clinging to my shoes and pants. I think about going across and coming back on the inside of the impoundment, but the walk does not look promising. I stop on the dike to photograph the pines and then continue the walk. After about ten minutes, I reach for my digital recorder. It is not in its usual place, nor anywhere else on my person. Searching my memory, I recall placing it on a stump for the photograph on the dike. But finding it may be the proverbial search for a needle in the haystack. I turn around and begin the search, looking for the place of the photograph. I recall that I was shooting pine trees, so that helps narrow the search. I finally see a likely place. I step up on the dike and see the stump with the recorder sitting there. I'm glad it will not be added to the other equipment I have lost on my travels in the past two years.

I take the fastest path on the return along the dike, across my homemade bridge and to the point. I cut across here, and with low tide I plan to cut across the little creek along the bank of Island Cut. *Kingfisher* is on the bank in the distance. The crossing appears muddy, and after two steps my right foot sinks, but I continue to step and make it to solid ground. The mud came up to the top of my shoe, but my sock was spared the pluff mud. After grabbing my stashed gear from the midden area, I take off my shoes and socks and sit by *Kingfisher* on the beach for lunch. It is a beautiful sunny afternoon, and after lunch the rising tide is directly under *Kingfisher*'s transom. The creek waters are lapping softly on the beach. A motorboat runs by, with the crew bundled up in contrast to my bare feet.

After stowing gear, I rig and shove off, an effortless task compared to my battle to get off the lee shore of Lighthouse Island last month. The wind is of variable strength, and at times we are going to windward well, but in lulls we are halted by the incoming tide. It is a struggle—when the wind dies I paddle to keep making way. Several boats pass, and I move out of the way. There is a fairly steady line of a ragtag fleet, all transporting the harvest of oysters to market.

We continue upwind and up-tide for twenty minutes, still not out of sight of Jeremy Island's beach, when my sponge goes overboard during a tack. There is a puff of wind, and I use the man-overboard drill of jibing, heading up and grabbing the sponge as a motorboat goes by. We wave, and they ask if I am all right. I yell, "Couldn't leave a good sponge—might need it later!" The outboard, "manned" by two women and a child, heads on and lands on the beach of Jeremy. Soon thereafter I have the thought, "Where are my muddy shoes?" They should be tied to the splash rail but are not; they must still be on Jeremy Island. So, after twenty-five minutes of work, we bear off with the wind and the tide for Jeremy. We quickly reach the beach and land up-tide as far as possible. My shoes are easy to find; I had tied them up on the cedar tree mooring. So we're off again, after the second retrieval of forgotten gear. It is a bit of a pattern, but I shake it off on the return sail, continuing to paddle through lulls.

The breeze is OK, and the procession of returning oyster-laden craft continues. I am impressed with how loaded they are and how tattered but utilitarian. The wind is finally steady in the last section of Clubhouse Creek before the turn to the ICW. A skiff is coming from behind. I am hugging the starboard bank, but he appears to want to cut this corner, so I give way to him. It is an old wooden bateau, with a huge pile of oysters and only inches of freeboard remaining. The waterman is an older African American man wearing a large gray sweatshirt with the hood up: both craft and man look weathered and ancient. He barely acknowledges my wave. He rounds the corner as we follow, going to windward, but now with the assistance of the incoming tide. Masts appear in the ICW. We arrive in the waterway, paralleling the course of a ketch close by. We make short tacks toward the channel to stay off the bank. After passing me, the ketch captain waves and hails, "At least you're sailing!" as he motors on. A multihull and then a trawler also pass heading south.

The sailing is not great since the wind is up and down. In working to pass the point into Jeremy Creek, I miscalculate the tide, and several more tacks are needed to make it in. The women and child I saw on Jeremy Island pass by, and then we make it into the creek. There is a waterman with his oyster-piled craft at the dock, and I wait for him to back his trailer and move his boat to the ramp before I land at the dock. A two-person crabber team comes in, dropping off one man to back down the trailer. I talk to them after they haul out. They were crabbing in all depths of water, and I see that they have done well, with a number of full bushel baskets. I back in my trailer and move *Kingfisher* off the dock to the ramp just as another crabber is coming in. I talk to him after he pulls out. Commenting on the familiar "bubbling" sound of his full bushels of crabs, he says it is the sound of money. He relates that he has not been crabbing much since the price of crabs has been low, but he is doing well now. He plans to crab until it gets cold.

After returning home and cleaning up *Kingfisher*, the large hickory trees stand out with beautiful golden fall foliage. The sunset continues the magnificent natural display: the red sky is not only the exclamation on this day but the herald of a trip to Bull Island tomorrow.

MILL ISLAND

Mill Island blends in to the quilt of marsh islands sitting behind the barriers of Cape Romain. To the eye it is indistinguishable from the green bodies of cordgrass between the waterways of the refuge. Like many marsh islands, a creek penetrates deep into the marsh interior, helping to alternately flood and drain this wetland. The island has some edges where a small rise in elevation has allowed the colonization by plants other than *Spartina alterniflora*. It seems a poor place to build a structure, and though it is hard to know what the island's elevation was like in the late eighteenth century, it still could not have stood much above high tides. Yet this was the location for a distinctive machine, particularly for this part of the world: a windmill for sawing timber.

At the time of the War for Independence, the Lynch family owned this marsh island, along with Cape Island and Raccoon Key. With the death of Thomas Lynch II, and then his son, Thomas Lynch III, who disappeared at sea, the property fell to the son's sister, Sabina Lynch. She married the Scottish immigrant John Bowman, and they resided at the Lynch plantation, Peachtree, on the South Santee River.

Bowman's behavior rated him an eccentric and a hothead. An account of one event reveals his temper—a conflict with his brother-in-law, Major James Hamilton. Like Bowman, Hamilton had moved into the area and married well (Bowman's wife's sister, Elizabeth), inheriting Orkland Plantation on the North Santee River. Bowman asserted that Hamilton had illegitimate

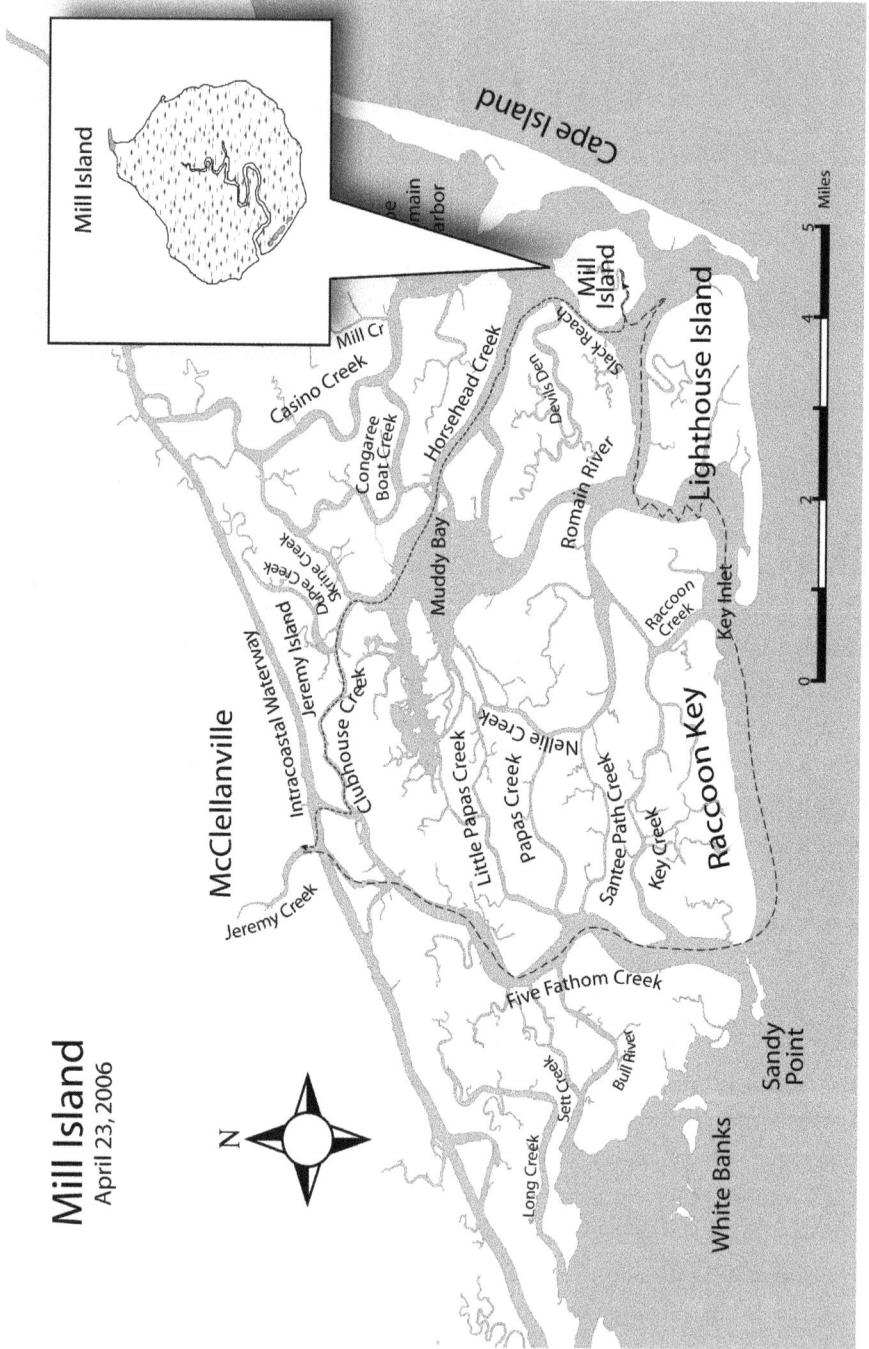

Mill Island

Mill Island

Cape Island

Mill Cr

Casino Creek

Congaree Boat Creek

Horsehead Creek

Devils Den

Slack Reach

Mill Island

Romain Harbor

Lighthouse Island

Muddy Bay

Romain River

Raccoon Creek

Key Inlet

Skrine Creek

Dupre Creek

Jeremy Island

Intracoastal Waterway

McClellanville

Clubhouse Creek

Little Papas Creek

Nellie Creek

Papas Creek

Santee Path Creek

Key Creek

Raccoon Key

Jeremy Creek

Five Fathom Creek

Sandy Point

Long Creek

Sett Creek

Bull River

White Banks

Mill Island
April 23, 2006

N

Miles
5
4
2
0

children in the North, and this attack provoked a duel between the two. The result was Hamilton's suffering a wound and loss of a leg. Henry Laurens complained that Bowman's "impoliteness" at his table insulted all those present. In his public service, Bowman was selected twice to the General Assembly, and he had the distinction of being the only Lowcountry planter to vote against the ratification of the federal Constitution in 1788. It is also said that Bowman avoided the tour of Washington through the Lowcountry for political reasons.

Bowman had ideas about improving the fortune he married into, and he contracted with Jonathan Lucas, immigrant from England and an experienced millwright, to build a water-driven rice mill at Peachtree plantation. This enterprise was a success for both men and initiated Lucas's career as a rice mill builder in the Lowcountry. Their next shared enterprise was the construction of a windmill for sawing timber, and the little island now known as Mill Island was selected for the building site. Earlier, Bowman had obtained a grant for fifteen marsh islands (including Mill), totaling 16,992 acres, all within the present borders of CRNWR. There is no historical evidence of selection rationale for Mill Island as the preferred site, but the following attributes probably played a role: positioning away from the mainland for maximum wind benefit, protection from coastal erosion, proximity to a major inlet for shipping timber (Cape Romain inlet), access to timber rafted down a river (South Santee) and proximity to Peachtree Plantation. The proximity to Peachtree was perhaps the least met of the needed location attributes. The location away from the mainland certainly created difficulties with its construction. Communication occurred via letters carried by sailing vessels, though Lucas ordered six passenger pigeons while working on the mill to further facilitate communication.

Evidence suggests that a windmill of Lucas's on Hog Island in Charleston Harbor was taken down, and the works were transported to Cape Romain for the construction of the Mill Island windmill. Bowman clearly saw an opportunity here that no one else had considered, or perhaps ever would. He also had something in mind when he sought title to the almost seventeen thousand acres of marsh islands in the refuge. Speculation can only help us consider what he had in mind—perhaps a windmill farm, anticipating those being built in the twenty-first century. The power of the wind was certainly used to transport the components from Hog Island in Charleston Harbor to Mill Island, including the five-ton iron wind shaft. The other required materials would also have been moved to the island by sail: timber, brick, canvas, etc., along with the workers. Leading this enterprise was Jonathan Lucas, whose occupation title—millwright—does not fully capture the intelligence and engineering abilities he possessed. Though no record is known of the accommodations for Lucas and his workers, we do know that his first son, William Lucas, was born on this site.

Lucas visualized and executed the construction of this machine with the capability of converting wind into the sawing of lumber. The outside of the completed mill had a conical tower of brick topped off with a wooden cap. Fixed sheds extended out to either side of the mill for the longitudinal sawing of the logs. Circling the body of the mill above the sheds was a wooden stage, where the miller with a mechanical device was able to rotate the cap to face the windmill's sails into the wind. These four sails of wood and canvas were fitted on the end of the wind shaft mounted through the mill's cap.

Inside the windmill, the mechanical works converted the turning of the sails into the sawing of logs. The rotation of the wind shaft and its brake wheel was transmitted to another gear wheel, the wallower, mounted on an upright shaft. From the lower part of this shaft, the crown wheel drove the crank wheel located on the crankshaft. On the bent projections of the crankshaft were fitted connecting rods attached to the vertical saw frames holding tensioned saw blades. The movement of the crankshaft created a reciprocating movement of the saw frames. Further mechanical apparatus enabled the sawmill to move the logs, along with a rolling carriage, by the windmill's power, as well as to tow the logs from the water along the slipway and onto the saw carriages.

One may speculate how residents would have reacted to this windmill when it was fully operational, with sails turning and logs sawing. Even though Mill Island is isolated from the mainland, surely there was wonder and amazement. The method of sawing logs into planks via the pit saw was slow and laborious. The contemporary local reaction would have been far different from the one that occurred at Limehouse in London in 1767: a new wind-powered sawmill was burned to the ground by a mob composed of hand-sawyers afraid of unemployment. It would not be long before steam engines revolutionized industry, and wind-powered sawmills became antiquities.

Mill Island

The Mill Island windmill operated for a while, but by 1822 it was without blades and posed a navigational hazard, appearing to some as resembling the Charleston lighthouse. The remains of the windmill, a collapsed brick mill tower and its iron works, lay on this site for years. Brick rubble still remains, but great amounts were clearly hauled off from this historical site. A group of people from McClellanville, led by Bud Hill from the Village Museum, recognized the historical value of the mill and sought to recover and conserve the mill shaft. Through the efforts of R.L. Morrison and Sons and Bob Baldwin, the shaft was extricated from the island and brought back to McClellanville, where it sat for a year at Carolina Seafood. The shaft finally was placed on display in front of the museum. The Village Museum went one step further, researching the windmill extensively and creating a working model, built by the local artist Lee Arthur. This meticulously crafted model resides in the museum but has the capability of being moved for display and demonstrations. The eighteenth-century windmill inspired these twenty-first-century efforts to remember and interpret.

APRIL 23, 2006

Low tide 10:50 a.m. Predicted winds NW 5–10 knots, then SW 10 knots.

This is my first launch from the new, improved Ashley Landing, a day I've been awaiting for three months. There are two vehicles and trailers at the landing at 8:05 a.m. when I arrive. We sail out Jeremy Creek at 8:25 a.m., and the nice northwest breeze is more than I anticipated. There is a strong outgoing tide for *Kingfisher* to ride heading out Five Fathom Creek. I'm still a bit paranoid about hitting fixed objects after the collision with a channel marker square on the bow in February, so I'm checking under the boom for pilings and other obstructions. There are no other boats around—our company is a *V* of cormorants passing overhead, flying north. Before long, we reach the confluence of Papas and Santee Path Creeks with Five Fathom, and the steady, moderate northwest breeze is perfect for running out into the bay and heading east for Key Inlet. My newly mounted compass on *Kingfisher's* splash rail is working well, and I am orienting to its swing.

I'm dressed in shorts and a T-shirt, and I pull on my personal flotation device (PFD) as I head out of the mouth of Five Fathom Creek to the bay/ocean. There is a boat in the old Five Fathom channel leading to the bay to the west as we get into open water at 9:30 a.m. The swell is small; after a jibe, our heading is due east, pointing directly at the lighthouses. I imagine what it would be like with large storm surf breaking where I now run parallel with Raccoon Key's shoreline. It is an easy reach for *Kingfisher*, and we soon pass the channel marked with floating buoys, headed to the south-southeast. We continue east, and I begin my search for a large offshore sandbar pointed out to me by Sarah Dawsey, refuge biologist, on a satellite image. There are glimpses of sand in the distance. Finally, I am close to the inlet and see the western tip of the beach of Lighthouse Island.

Shoals begin to appear around my projected course, and rather than run out around the shoals and lose my windward gauge, I search to find a small channel for *Kingfisher* to squeeze through. The large sandbar on the shore side is connected to Raccoon Key. It is getting quite shallow, and after raising the daggerboard I soon must pull it all the way out. The rudder is now kicking up, and despite my best efforts to locate a trough, *Kingfisher* is soon grounded. I step out and begin pulling *Kingfisher* over the shoal, encouraged by the sight of clear, deep water a short distance ahead. Now the depth is just a couple of inches, and the pulling includes a bit of dragging the hull over the bar. The tide is still falling, so it is no time to tarry.

We are finally through and sailing again. Standing to survey the inlet, there is no magical new sand island, but there is a large area of shoals to the south with small surf breaking on it. A bit of a channel stretches out to the southwest, and I store this knowledge for future use. The waters of the inlet inside of the shoals are smooth. I decide to stop off for a quick look on the west end of what was South Cape Island. This is my second time on this isle, having surveyed the beach for new turtle nests this past summer with Matt Connolly, CRNWR manager. Farther up the backside of the island, another boat has already landed. The steep drop-off on the point makes for an easy landing. I leave the sail up and take a walk around, heading over to the marked "Closed Area." I heard during my hatchery building in April from a fellow volunteer, Billy Warren, about the hard work in putting these signs up. There is no sign of the feathered denizens of this closed area, so it is time to cast off on *Kingfisher* again.

Mill Island

We head out into the inlet and note ahead, at Raccoon Creek, where a boat roars out toward the barrier island. Least terns are working in these waters. There is still a little outgoing tide, and on the backside of Lighthouse Island two boats have landed. The creek, heading in from the inlet, turns to the north. We are sailing to windward and progressing slowly. We hold a tack on the western side too long and run aground. On the other tack, and going slowly, it is apparent that we have come to a stop, and despite the lack of any sound, the daggerboard must be in the soft mud. So we play the middle of the creek by making more frequent tacks. A couple in a boat just departed from the beach passes by. I notice the mouth of a creek to the east cutting into the island.

It is taking a while to tack past the point of Lighthouse Island due to the diminishing wind. We are finally past and now closehauled, heading toward the Romain River. All through this area, the lighthouses have remained the predominant visual markers. At the next point of the island and the waters of the Romain River, I bear off and recognize the waterway to Muddy Bay, where in the previous month I came through on *Island Cat*, the multihull ferry of Coastal Expeditions. I was warned about the water depth here. A mud flat sits in the center of this waterway, and I take the northern channel, following the crab pots. Water depth has decreased on the chart, and staying on the north side, I soon find myself in shallow water. The daggerboard drags and soon must be pulled up; then the rudder kicks up and is dragging. I get out and pull *Kingfisher* by walking across this muddy bottom toward the channel. Grass and clams are underfoot in the mud.

Making it back to deep water, I follow the crab pots again. The tide is low, and the wind has become variable. We run aground on the Lighthouse Island side. I stand and look for both Slack Creek and the high ground on Mill Island. Ahead, the surface of the water comes alive, and it is the beginning of the south-southwest breeze. I am close to the landing area on Lighthouse Island and look over to Mill Island for the signs of a creek entrance. There are only a couple of little patches of high ground on Mill. Soon the shallowness appears everywhere, and I conclude that I have missed the entrance to Slack Reach. We tack back in the search and again find mud flats. With the board and rudder kicked up, and no channel found, we are aground. Accepting this state, I pull out lunch and eat while slightly scraping along. Earlier, I had thought about eating lunch on the beach at Cape Island, but now I relax, waiting for the tide to come in to help. Gene Morrison, a local commercial and now recreational fisherman, calls this area the Romain Mudflat rather than the Romain River.

A boat appears coming out of Slack Reach in the distance, moving fast in deep water, but soon its progress stops upon finding the shallow waters. We are again moving and head to the point sprouting an interesting steel structure used in commercial clamming, adjacent to which the entrance to the creek penetrates into Mill Island. The tide is still exceedingly low, and the entrance seems equally shallow. I decide to turn *Kingfisher* in and use my paddle to help get the bow pointed in the right direction, since the water depth is still too shallow for the rudder to provide any help. We scrape through, and once in the blind creek, I notice deeper water, allowing the luxury of daggerboard and rudder use.

It is good sailing, despite the fact that the banks of the creek are high due to the low tide. Soon after we enter the creek, small turtles pile off the bank to starboard and plop into the water. These can be none other than Carolina diamondback terrapins (*Malaclemys terrapin centrata*). This is the only U.S. turtle to inhabit estuaries, coastal rivers and mangrove swamps and to range from fresh to salt water. Their populations have been greatly reduced, with a major decline in the twentieth century. They were earlier hunted for the making of terrapin soups and stews, but their recent decline is in part due to the by-catch of the blue crab industry—both commercial and recreational. Terrapins go into either baited or un-baited traps, and when they are not able to exit, they drown. "Ghost" or derelict crab traps are now seen as hazardous refuse for these reptiles.

(I was to get a close-up look at a very young terrapin the following year on Cape Island. A friend of Jerry Tupacz, seasonal biologist for the turtle program, brought the little turtle to him after finding it on a trip to North Island. The friend mistakenly thought it was a loggerhead hatchling. Jerry released the little turtle on the backside of Cape Island on that April day, hoping it would have a go at it in the refuge.)

I am close to my objective for this voyage: finding the remains of the windmill on this mainly marsh island. I previously learned that the remains—brick rubble—were located on high ground on the southwest side, but I can only see marsh. Timbers protrude from the bank to starboard, but no high ground is to be seen, even when standing in the cockpit. One section of the bank has a covering of different vegetation—glassworts—but nothing more. We sail on in the creek, going deeper into this island of mostly cordgrass, which does not seem a great foundation for any structure, much less a windmill. Continuing through a series of bends, and starting to shift to sail more off the wind, a bend to the west alerts me that we have gone too far and it is time to abort this search and turn around. Now we beat against the south-southwest wind, and the tide is rolling in the creek against us. There is not much room to tack and gain headway, and we find the creek banks when the daggerboard hits mud, considerably slowing our progress. We battle to claw out of this creek and finally round a bend where we aren't beating to windward. *Kingfisher* is on a reach and retracing the course.

In the final section, while passing the glasswort section and acting on a hunch, I land *Kingfisher* on the mud bank with glassworts and pull the hull up, noticing that the black mud is firm. I scramble up the bank, finding the top to also be firm. From this higher perspective, the vegetation of higher ground appears close to the Romain River. A paddle pushed into the mud bank becomes the temporary mooring for *Kingfisher*, and after the bow line is fast, I begin the walk across about fifty yards of marsh, squishing along with neoprene socks covered with sandals. I cross to the nearest section, and while walking along the edge of this higher ground and marsh, I find some scattered brick rubble. Moving on to the next section of high ground, I spot a substantial amount of brick. Brick rubble is scattered throughout the middle of the vegetation on the high ground and down the bank by the Romain River. Somewhere near here the five-ton iron shaft of the mill lay neglected prior to recovery and display at the Village Museum.

Wondering about this recovery, I head back to *Kingfisher*, imagining views of an adrift craft floating downwind and down-tide in the creek. Reassured by the sight of the sail coming across the marsh, I end up on the wrong side of a little creeklet dividing the glasswort section from the predominant *Spartina* marsh. Nonchalantly stepping across the rivulet with camera in one hand, the softer pluff mud swallows a sandal, and I find myself on one foot, with a sandal sucked under and oysters all around. Sticking the camera in a pocket, I gingerly step back to retrieve and replace the sandal while precariously balanced on one foot.

Carefully crossing back, I make the final steps to *Kingfisher* and pull out the paddle with some effort due to the mud's suction. While washing off the paddle, I notice that both my sponges are gone—I assume casualties of the landing process. Without a sponge, I wash off the sandals as best as possible and tie them to the spray rail, completing the coarse cleanup by washing off the wet suit socks still on my feet. To stay out of the mud, I push *Kingfisher* back into the creek while sitting on the bow. I begin the little trick of walking around the mast but miscalculate and find the craft heeling sharply to windward. Before the point of no return, I drop off into the water up to my armpits to prevent capsize, catching onto the deck to keep from going farther. I pull my soaking body into the cockpit, straighten up the mess and get sailing. The water actually feels refreshing rather than cold after my recent exertions, though any onlookers would have had quite a chuckle over the maneuver worthy of Buster Keaton.

We now reach the mouth of the creek and, with flooding tide, are easily out without a scrape. I utilize the same power that Bowman and Lucas did to run the machine that was used to saw trees in the late eighteenth century. We steer toward the northwest, looking for a channel in Slack Reach ahead, and when clear, we jibe with a new course to the northeast. Crab pot buoys are useful to help guide the way. Running out past a fisherman working the west side of Mill Island, we jibe into Horsehead Creek. It is a pristine view to the northeast toward Cowpen Point, a most familiar landing in my trips with the turtle conservation team. A solid incoming tide is helping push my wind machine *Kingfisher* along on this great beam reach. The wind has increased to pull us home. Farther along, the landmarks of pine forest on Cape Island and the lighthouses astern are becoming distant. Ahead is another vertical landmark—an old metal observation tower. We're passing Horsehead Island now, one of the few marsh islands named on the chart, deriving its name from either the shape of the island or the figure of a bush there. Past the observation tower and another small marsh island, we are out into Muddy Bay. It is a closer reach, and wetter, with increased wind and chop on this more open body of water. The compass is coming in handy in setting this course, looking for the entrance to the creek where we departed and where I entered on *Island Cat* the previous month. Finding it, we bear off and, in passing the entrance to Skrine Creek, notice the anchored wooden craft that has been converted into someone's home. It appears that a person is moving onboard, but on closer inspection it is two brown pelicans roosting on deck.

Bearing off into Island Cut, we come through the marsh and pass Jeremy Island. A small beach appears to be a very good landing spot, and some signs of shell midden are evident. The creek turns to the west, and we're beating and opposed by the reversed incoming tide. Several boats with young people are out in the creek, enjoying this warm April day. It is slow progress, but the steady wind helps with moving forward. We slip the bonds of this creek in the turn to the north toward the ICW and finally into Jeremy Creek. The landing is now full of a fleet of trucks with boat trailers as I land and haul my craft away.

LIGHTHOUSE ISLAND

This island, like many of those surrounding it, has been in transit for all of its recorded history. The island was historically included as part of the larger Raccoon Key, a low-lying island with the beach facing south toward the merging waters of Bulls Bay and the Atlantic Ocean. Earlier maps indicated that the land was the Raccoon Keys, divided by a tidal creek. These divisions have increased since those early maps, with the largest waterway now separating Raccoon Key from the present Lighthouse Island. This creek, an extension of Key Inlet, would seem to naturally have been named Key Creek, yet this name was already given to the creek forming the back boundary of Raccoon Key. The present Lighthouse Island is defined by this extension of Key Inlet on the west; the Romain River to the north, turning around into the waters of Cape Romain harbor to the east; and the marsh and small creek to the south that separates Lighthouse from Cape Island. But this is the view on the NOAA chart of 1980. Recent satellite views show that the bottom projection to the west of Cape Island has separated from the main island and has now welded onto Lighthouse Island. This section was formerly called South Cape Island, but now both DNR and USFWS call this barrier Lighthouse Island. I suspect that the movement and renaming of these islands will be an ongoing process.

Even with the welded barrier island, Lighthouse is predominately salt marsh. The main area of upland is on the northeastern side and is where the two lighthouses were built. This location is currently well back from the ocean, but historically the beach was close to the lighthouses, with earlier sand dunes now

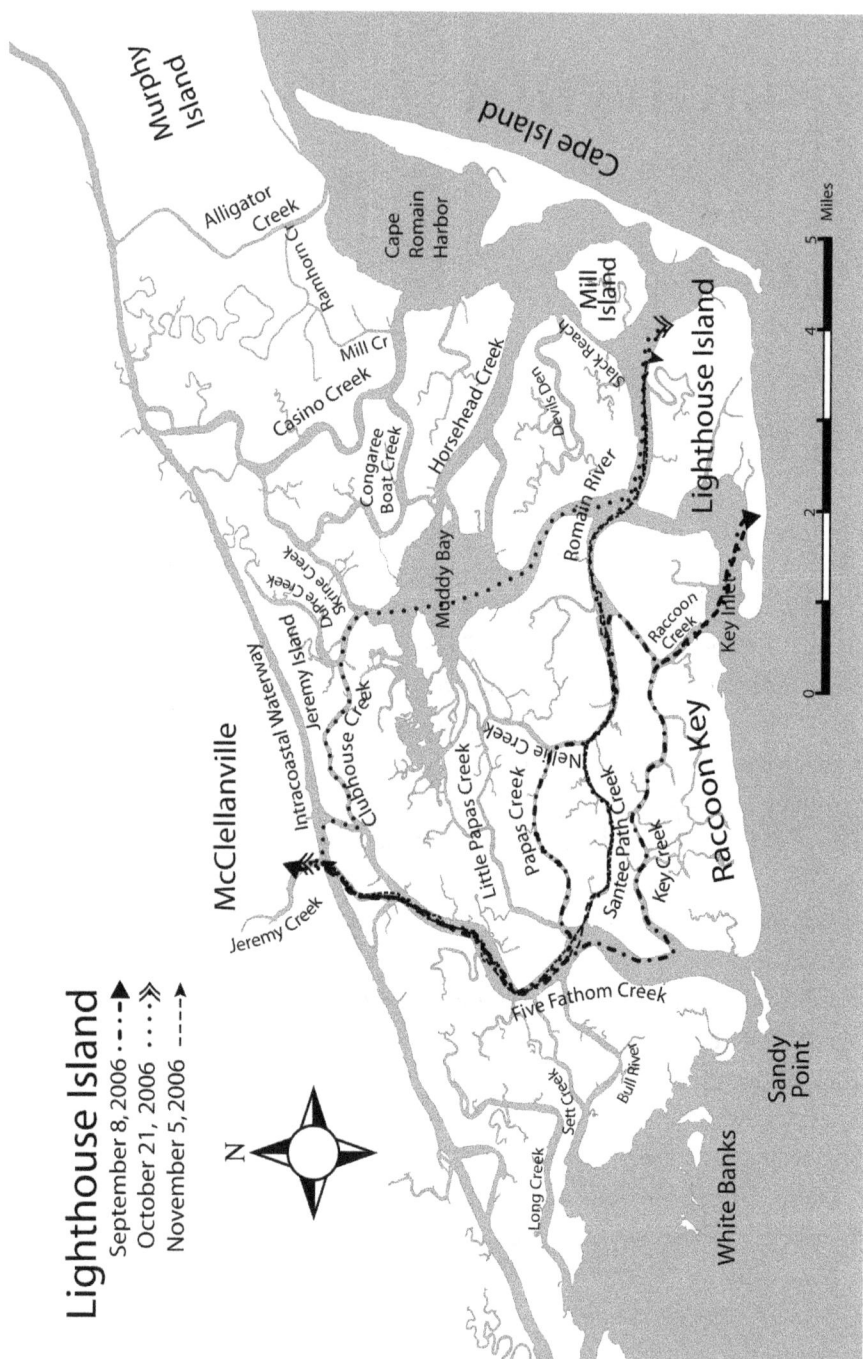

Murphy Island

Alligator Creek

Ranhorn Cr

Mill Cr

Casino Creek

Congaree Boat Creek

Horsehead Creek

Cape Romain Harbor

Cape Island

Mill Island

Slack Reach

Devils Den

Romain River

Lighthouse Island

Raccoon Creek

Key Inlet

Muddy Bay

Skrine Creek

Dupre Creek

Jeremy Island

Intracoastal Waterway

Clubhouse Creek

Little Papas Creek

Papas Creek

Nellie Creek

Santee Path Creek

Key Creek

Raccoon Key

McClellanville

Jeremy Creek

Five Fathom Creek

Sett Creek

Bull River

Long Creek

White Banks

Sandy Point

Lighthouse Island
September 8, 2006
October 21, 2006
November 5, 2006

N

0   1   2   3   4   5   Miles

extensively covered by colonizing vegetation. A stand of pine trees presently lies between the lighthouses and the wetlands in the direction of the ocean, balancing the pine forest on Cape Island to the northeast. A large segment of the vegetation on this upland is invasive species, many reflecting the human occupation here. Chinaberry pokes above the riot of vines, splashed in spring with the purple of rampant wisteria. There was also deliberate cultivation of other botanical species by lighthouse keepers and their families: Hannah, the second wife of the lighthouse keeper Augustus F. Wichmann, planted an apple tree on the island, along with orange trees from seed.

Part of the Lighthouse Island complex of upland and wetlands are a couple of narrow hammocks stretched off of the main upland toward the west, appearing on satellite images as a thin wishbone. With only a narrow, shallow creek separating this wishbone from the main island upland, these thin isles in the marsh certainly qualify as hammocks and are dominated by red cedar, wax myrtle and yaupon holly.

The number of shipwrecks along the Cape Romain area was an incentive for the federal government to consider the establishment of a lighthouse to warn mariners of the dangerous Cape Romain shoals reaching out several miles off the shore. The following is one account from 1759:

On the 25th ult. [October 25, 1759] the Ship Judith, Capt. Arno, of and for Falmouth, from Cape Fear, with about 200 Barrels of Pitch, Tar, etc. went ashore on Cape Romain, and was entirely lost. The Crew saved

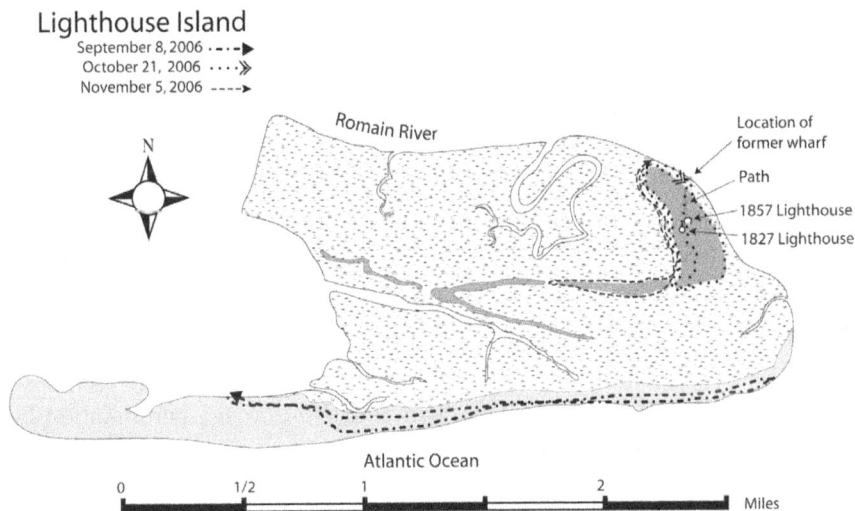

Lighthouse Island

September 8, 2006
October 21, 2006
November 5, 2006

Romain River

Location of former wharf

Path

1857 Lighthouse

1827 Lighthouse

N

Atlantic Ocean

0   1/2   1   2   Miles

themselves in the Ship's boat, and underwent great Hardships before they got here [Charleston]*; three of them perished on a small Island or Key near the Cape.*

The location of the small island where these three men perished is unknown. These small sand islands regularly grow and deconstruct, and we can only wonder about the men's ultimately fruitless efforts to survive.

While the old mill on Mill Island was considered as a base for the light, it was ruled out as insufficient. This mill tower on Mill Island caused some confusion, appearing during the day like a lighthouse, and one instance in particular led to the loss of a vessel. In 1816, the Spanish schooner *Diamante* was bound from Havana, Cuba, to the west coast of Africa. This was either a slaving or pirate voyage; the size of the crew (fifty-one) fit either endeavor. The slave trade had been abolished, and the men would have been prepared to fight if slaving was their mission. They were in distress after being dismasted in a gale and recruited the help of a schooner, taking onboard a Captain Gardner. His task was to pilot them in to Charleston. He mistook the Mill Island tower for the Charleston lighthouse and eventually put the *Diamante* on the Cape Romain shoals. A number of the crew perished.

The federal government finally approved funds in 1823 for the building of a lighthouse. Cape Island was considered for the building site, but its low elevation and exposure to the sea was ruled out in favor of the east end of Raccoon Key. With the land purchased, the contractor selected Winslow Lewis, who had much experience in building lighthouses. The sixty-five-foot conical tower was finished in 1827 and originally was painted black and white. The base of the conical tower's diameter was 29.5 feet, and the top diameter was 15.0 feet. A residence for the keeper was built at the same time of solid brick. The cost for the tower and house was $7,475. Lewis had also developed his own lamp and reflector system, and the cost for the installation of the lighting was $950. At some point after the construction of the second lighthouse, the first tower was painted red and mainly used for storage.

Even after the construction of this first light, there was still, at times, confusion, with several vessels thinking it was the Charleston light. On December 2, 1832, the large American ship *Pennsylvania*, commanded by Captain Patterson and bound from Le Havre, France, to Pennsylvania, went ashore on the outer shoal of Cape Romain. Similar to the ship *Coriolanus* a few weeks earlier, the *Pennsylvania* had confused the Cape Romain lighthouse with the Charleston light. Unlike the *Coriolanus*, which was able to get off after running aground, the *Pennsylvania*'s crew cut away first her mizzenmast and then her mainmast—to no avail—trying to save the ship. With a strong northeast gale blowing, the *Pennsylvania* and her cargo were a total loss, with the loss of at least one passenger. The ship had onboard 105 crew and passengers (Swiss émigrés).

Despite the government and human efforts in this project, the outcome of the first Cape Romain lighthouse was an insufficient beacon for warning ships. Though a new lamp system was installed in 1847, the lighthouse board decided that a taller and more powerful light was needed. The new lighthouse was completed in 1857 not far from the original light. The new tower, built with slave labor, was octagonal in section and 150 feet tall. Originally, the tower's exterior finish was left as natural brick, but later the bottom half was painted white and the top half, black and white. Dwellings for the lighthouse keepers, a wick house and a boathouse were also constructed. The light was a first-order Fresnel lens and shone for the first time on January 1, 1858. The lighthouse included an interior spiral staircase to access the lamp house, a revolving lamp platform, an exterior balcony with an iron railing and a circular brass roof. This lighthouse was not without flaws. Cracks appeared in the coming years, the west side of the foundation settled and eventually the tower leaned two feet from the vertical. In 1937, the light was automated, and it was finally deactivated in 1947, as lighted buoys were placed directly on the dangerous offshore shoals.

When the light was deactivated, the keeper's dwelling houses and other support buildings were torn down. In poor repair and vandalized, the lighthouses continued to deteriorate until the leadership of McClellanville native Tommy Graham organized friends and family in a renovation effort. This project was instrumental in stabilizing and securing these important historical structures. The difficult logistics of working in such an isolated area were surmounted in replacing the lamp house glazing and painting the exterior of the 150-foot tower. Much still needs to be done; at present, the stairs are not safe for the public to ascend to the grand view of the surrounding area. Plans for further work and the application for federal funds have been made. The lighthouses have gained further protection by their placement on the National Register of Historic Places in 1980. Besides the ravage of the elements, human damage continues, as was evident on a

2007 trip to the lighthouse for USFWS volunteers. The bottom door of the lighthouse had been broken in a forced entry, and the second-floor door allowing entry to the stairwell was also damaged.

I learned about the longest-serving keeper on the island, Augustus F. Wichmann, from his son, Fred Wichmann. Augustus, born in 1868, was an immigrant from Germany. He got into the lighthouse service after serving in the Spanish-American War. Wichmann ran into an officer in Charleston who offered him a job. He initially started on the bottom rung of the lighthouse service, rowing from buoy to buoy on the Savannah River to keep the lamps burning. He became an assistant keeper at Hunting Island and was there for the hurricane of 1911. He was promoted to keeper at the Cape Romain lighthouse and served there for twenty-one years. In the hurricane of 1926, a tug towing two coal barges north was wrecked on Raccoon Key. He went to the rescue and rowed a small boat across the inlet to reach Raccoon Key. The storm surf covered the beach on this barrier island, and at times Wichmann had to wade due to the high surf and tide. Augustus found the exhausted captain of one of the barges, the 110-foot schooner *Northwest*, and proceeded to carry him on his back. After this superhuman effort, and one more row across the inlet to Lighthouse Island, he made it back to shelter— all told, an ordeal of fourteen hours.

Wichmann's wife, Hannah, died on the island in 1928, and the next year an uncommon romance blossomed. While traveling to the lighthouse during a Cape Island party, twenty-one-year-old Hazel Wyndham caught the eye of Augustus, forty years her senior, and the following year they married. The husband and wife's recreation on the island included racing up the lighthouse steps, a race that Augustus always won. Hazel became pregnant and was due on February 20, 1930. Dr. Edward McClellan and a black midwife, Hessie, were on the island for the delivery. After a night awaiting the event, Augustus persuaded the doctor to go fishing at dawn. Upon their return after a few hours, Augustus proudly showed Hessie a twenty-five-pound bass. Hessie responded by showing her "catch": a baby boy.

This infant was Fred Wichmann, who for some time was an only child on the island. The isolation was so profound that he thought he was the only child on earth until he ran into other children on a trip to McClellanville. A younger brother soon followed on the island. Fred Wichmann recalled at age three falling on "coon" oysters at the Lighthouse Island landing and fainting from the bleeding. The next year, 1934, his father retired from the lighthouse service, and they moved off the island.

Goats were placed on the island in the past to keep the underbrush down, but since they were nonnative, these animals were removed. The vegetation has gone riot in the area around the lighthouses. The Romain River has continued to become shallower, only admitting craft at certain tides. Entry onto the island is at best a muddy slog, and outgoing tides can easily capture the unwary boater. While the towers have been stabilized, considerable work is needed for a complete renovation.

SEPTEMBER 8, 2006

Low tide 3:30 p.m. Predicted winds NE 10–15 knots.

I am easily out and going with the chugging outgoing tide at 10:45 a.m. *Kingfisher* has required a couple of repairs prior to setting out, but the traveler needs re-rigging on the fly. The sail out is undisturbed by boat traffic and accentuated by an osprey's crossing and the exhalation of a dolphin. Fair weather cumulus clouds provide bas-relief for a bright blue sky. The destination today is the barrier island formerly known as South Cape Island, the narrow remnant barrier with a west–east axis created by the dividing of Cape Island by the breach in 1996. This barrier is now considered part of Lighthouse Island. The plan is to sail out via Five Fathom Creek, Papas Creek, Nellie Creek, the Romain River and the creek to Key Inlet, landing on the backside of the island. From here, a walk to the east end and back will be the land part of the journey prior to the return sail. The planned course out will require a passage through Papas Creek against the outgoing tide, though I could head out into Bulls Bay.

After the easy sail down Five Fathom Creek, we make the turn into the entrance to Papas Creek, and the strong outgoing tide is a force. With some work, we finally make it into this creek. The creek's direction changes directly into the wind, and our beat to windward begins. Each tack is a loser, with lost headway meaning lost ground with the tide's surge and constant sideways slippage. We use the full extent of the creek width and the slightly slower flow along the bank's edge before each tack, literally contacting the *Spartina* in the tacking process. The occasional squawk of a great blue heron and the blow of a dolphin add to the atmosphere of the creek drama. The creek's name, Papas, is derived from the Gullah pronunciation of "porpoise."

The drama is not going well for forward progress and leads to the contemplation of another course to our destination: out Five Fathom Creek into the Bay and then into Key Inlet. I had not anticipated such a battle due to the strength of this outgoing tide in this creek. The *Myth of Sisyphus* comes to mind—rolling the huge boulder up the long incline and then having it come rolling back down to start all over. The defects in my sail and the numerous nicks and dings in the daggerboard are drags on this effort, where every little disturbance in the flow is keeping *Kingfisher* from pushing through this bottleneck.

I try to hold *Kingfisher* on the port tack closehauled near the marsh, working to squeeze through, and instead find us embraced by the marsh grass. I extricate us from this hold and continue the battle as dolphins cruise by, perhaps wondering what all the fuss is about. We are moving better now in the changed course of the last section prior to Nellie Creek. An oystercatcher makes an appearance before we bear off into Nellie Creek to join the outgoing tide, and the sudden change in progress is truly liberating after an hour-and-a-half struggle. The boulder is now rolling down the hill in the right direction. We sail past the entrance to the Santee Path Creek to starboard and come up again to closehauled while entering the Romain River. Several small outboards pass us as we continue the beat with the luxury of the accompanying outgoing tide. Along the bank there is a manmade structure of poles and wire for clamming. I look for the branch of the creek that will head southwest prior to the entrance to Raccoon Creek leading to Key Inlet. We finally bear off and are now running into this waterway on a jog away from the direct course to the destination.

The opening in the marsh revealing Raccoon Creek appears ahead to the south, and continuing on toward the west is Key Creek. We make the jibe into Raccoon Creek and are now reaching through this fairly narrow waterway. Ahead, a blotch of white marks our destination: the west end of the beach of Lighthouse Island. Coming out of the creek into the wide body of water known as Key Bay, I note to starboard the end of my walk on Raccoon Key in May. The operator of a small outboard that passed me earlier has his boat on the bank and is walking across the substantial sand spit. *Kingfisher* is closehauled while crossing this shallow bay of the inner inlet in fairly smooth water. There are no boats ahead to the backside of this narrow barrier island, and I search for a landing where *Kingfisher* can be properly secured. Making a landing and dropping sail, I walk the boat up the beach, haul her up the sand a little and secure the mooring line to something solid. There is still about an hour and a half of outgoing tide, but it is later than I had planned to do the end-to-end walk. In the interest of time, I will make the crossing to the beach before heading east. Grabbing my pack, I head off, eating lunch on the fly.

There is some width to the island here, and the area behind the dunes has standing water and is littered with shells. Before heading over to the beach, I walk along the backside of the island and see that it ends in marsh that extends all the way to the dunes. There is a little track prior to the end of walkable land on the island's backside, and I follow this around until there are two clear tracks from an ATV. Through some standing water, an army of fiddler crabs moves as a unit away from my encroachment. The ATV is located to my left. I traveled on an ATV here with Refuge Manager Matt Connolly the previous year while doing one of the daily turtle surveys. Today, I am on foot and alone. Once across, a washed-up crab pot provides a good landmark for finding this track on the return trip.

No new ATV tracks appear today on the beach. There are no footprints either, and it is clear that I am alone on the island. Trawlers are offshore, working in the same area as on the previous Sunday. Dunes reside in the first section of beach encountered, but just ahead is an area of extensive overwash without dunes, with sand reaching into the marsh on the island's backside. Gulls idle along the shoreline in groups. Sea purslane covers a small mound of sand, and this plant appears to be performing its role of colonizing and creating the beginning of a dune. Some areas along here have no vegetation; they are merely sand and shell in a flat ridge. Back in the marsh, a creek winds through the cordgrass. This creek and marsh are the dividing point between this barrier island and the inner island that are now welded together like two colliding continents. Gene Morrison shared with me that there used to be no marsh here, just open water. While continental collisions take a much longer time, the changes here resulting in a segment of Cape Island becoming part of Lighthouse Island have occurred in decades.

An upland spine of Lighthouse Island appears to stretch on the southern side of the island toward the west-northwest, with isolated hammocks topped with cedars dotting this end. This spine is separate from the high ground of the main part of the island where the lighthouses stand on its northeast side. Pine forest is taking hold on the southeast end of the spine, similar to the stand on Cape Island's upland. As I walk, I pass a landmark: an isolated yucca stand, in front of which a kayak is chained to a buried pipe. This must be the old kayak used to cross the inlet at Cape Point for the loggerhead management program, until that practice was deemed unsafe. On the beach ahead are areas of exposed backbarrier muddy sediments, and shorebirds are probing for invertebrates. Not far beyond is a shallow tidal creek cutting through the beach. I crossed it the previous year and wonder about the water depth today, but since it is almost low tide it is only several inches. Ahead are exposed shoals in the inlet, with breakers on the ocean and shoals beyond. The maritime display is stunning to behold. Past the shallow water crossing the beach, there is some size to its source creek in the marsh. Metal cages marked by spray-painted PVC pipe protect several loggerhead turtle nests along this walk. Toward the east end of the island, a fine high set of dunes provide for excellent 360-degree views. At the inlet, I survey this side of the shoreline and inlet, reflecting on passing in and out of this area the past Sunday. The water is much shallower than when I passed through on Sunday, and the shoals I cut across to round the point are now an extensive exposed sandbar.

I am tempted to continue the walk around the end of the island to the backside but must turn around, as I am beginning to push the limits of the return sail. With a quick turn, I am on the move, with camera holstered. Trawlers continue to work offshore. I follow my previous footprints, walking into the sun. The tide is now out, and the change to incoming will assist me once in Five Fathom Creek. The walk is quicker than the one out, and the only stop I make is for an unsuccessful close-up of an uncooperative fiddler crab army. On the island's backside, *Kingfisher* is alone and secure. My weathered Teva sandals have held together until now, when the lower and upper soles begin to separate. The final walk has a rhythm of flapping from the failed footwear. If this is the only gear failure for the day, it will be most successful. There are signs that the breeze is stronger than upon the earlier landing.

Lighthouse Island

I quickly work to untether *Kingfisher*, secure gear and get the craft to the water. On the course home, we'll hit Key Creek and make a passage west until we reach Five Fathom Creek and then Jeremy Creek. I feel the anxiety of making a passage through a creek with which I am not familiar, but with no one around to ask I must trust the experience of seeing boats roaring into the creek from the Five Fathom Creek end. The source of my anxiety is clear: my recent nightmare passage through Joe and Ben Creek. After the sail is up and sheeted in, we are off on a starboard reach across the inner inlet, and a quick jump up onto a plane indicates that the wind strength is about fifteen knots. There is some water to cover before entering Raccoon Creek and finally meeting up with the wider creek ahead. We bear off and run into this passage, and the chart indicates (for what it is worth) that at low tide the depth of Key Creek is five feet here and at the other end, eight feet. I refuel with some Gatorade and a banana. The chart is a useful navigation aid since there are occasional branches to lead one astray. This waterway forms the northern boundary of Raccoon Key. The low tide has our profile in the creek quite low, and even when standing I can just see the tops of *Spartina* extending on both sides. There are more commercial fishing structures along the banks.

We are making good progress with the following wind, winding through a few bends, but I detect the beginning of the incoming tide opposed to our course. The chart shows a sunken vessel along here, but there is no sign of it. Dolphins come up to starboard but do not approach. Ahead there appears some type of manmade structure above the marsh, and I imagine it is a range marker in Five Fathom Creek. Several creeks veer off into the marsh toward a small open area labeled on the chart as Key Bay. Soon the structure seen earlier appears as the upper works of a trawler anchored in the middle of the creek, the *Voile D*. She has her booms still out wide with nets up, and I jibe and head to the port side of the creek since there appears to be more room. Passing close abeam, I scan the deck for the crew, but no one is stirring. The crewmen appear to be breaking for the evening from trawling and have anchored here rather than returning to port. Astern of the trawler now, I am startled by a dolphin duo rising up to starboard within arm's length. The closer of the two leaves a calling card with the smack of his tail on the water, wetting me with a good splash.

This is not my first close encounter with these powerful, intelligent and wild marine mammals. After one episode in which a dolphin bursting from below the surface and exhaling within an arm's length startled me into yelling out loud, I empathized more readily with one of Nathaniel Bishop's greatest anxieties in his two-thousand-mile journey down the coast: the threat to his paper canoe by "gamboling porpoises." I interpret this dolphin behavior as play. I recall seeing a photograph of a pod of dolphins playing "catch" with a cannonball jellyfish. One of the dolphins was doing a tail stand and balancing the "ball" on its snout before hurling it for the others to chase after. Gene Morrison told a story of being offshore and seeing the same game underway, but with a different "ball." A dolphin had grabbed a small octopus from below, and with the animal pulling itself in tightly to a round shape, the game was on.

Dolphins are common in the Cape Romain area. In the fieldwork for her master's thesis, Peggy Sloan, a staff member from the North Carolina Aquarium, spent two years studying the bottlenose dolphin (*Tursiops truncatus*) in the area. She used a standard method of identifying the dolphins: photo-identification focused on dorsal fin scars, allowing for recognition of individuals. A catalog exists for specific dolphins from Cape May, New Jersey, to central Florida. There are some holes in the South Carolina database that Sloan targeted. Her study looked at the residency patterns, seasonality and habitat use of the Cape Romain dolphins. She identified 121 individuals. In this group, 22 were deemed to be year-round residents, 49 were seasonal residents and 50 were transients. In comparing these dolphins to those in the coastal catalog, 11 dolphins were known from other areas. The year-round residents were always seen in the salt marsh and not the ocean. Those dolphins seen feeding around shrimp trawlers were exclusively transients.

Shortly, the waters of Key and Five Fathom Creek join, and a jibe has *Kingfisher* headed home. The strong incoming tide favors progress. Past channel marker #12, the creek's turn to the north-northeast brings us back up to closehauled, and it appears the next point can be made without a tack. The tide assists laying this point, and we bear off now in the bend to the northwest. The entrance to my previous Papas ordeal lies off to starboard, and the experience seems like it occurred long ago. That plagued passage is in contrast to the present reach, and soon we are rounding up in the next strong bend to the northeast. No other boats share this waterway. Our great progress will have us in much earlier than anticipated. *Kingfisher* is closehauled as I hike out flat at times and occasionally use the deck cleats for a break in holding the sheet. As we pass another channel marker, I notice that the velocity of the tide is impressive, with water rushing by the piling. In Town Creek, we're closehauled again. In the distance I first hear and then see a motorboat in the ICW. With the craft's wake revealing a shoal ahead, we tack once, holding it all the way across the creek, and then tack back for the last tack of the day.

Slipping into Jeremy Creek, the high bank to starboard is a barrier to the wind flow and slows down progress. With a final rounding up to windward and dropping of the sail, we coast into the landing at the dock. An outboard is concurrently dropping in the ramp, and the fisherman states that he is going to fish Shark Point in Muddy Bay. The length of the passage from my landing point on Lighthouse Island to Jeremy Creek was one and a half hours, the time it took to make the earlier passage through Papas Creek. As the fisherman heads out, *Kingfisher* is the last craft at the landing. A man with long hair and a beard, drinking a beer and coming to check out the landing after work, strikes up a conversation with me. Pete recalls some Sunfish sailing from his past, particularly one instance when he vainly tried to make it past the point at the mouth of Jeremy Creek in sight of the landing. He could not clear it for what seemed like an eternity due to the opposing wind and tide. We share a laugh about the challenges of sailing small boats and head our separate ways.

October 21, 2006

Low tide 2:30 p.m. Predicted winds NE 15 knots,
then NE 10–15 knots in the afternoon.

We are rigged and preparing to cast off at 8:50 a.m. A Georgetown guide's party of two at the dock offers the cast off. With thanks, we take the breeze heading out Jeremy Creek to the ICW. At home on my deck before dawn, the starry sky had featured the Twins and Orion, and now the sky is clear without a cloud. Once out of the ICW and into the entrance to Clubhouse Creek, passing by "peeps" on a shell rake, the morning can best be described as delicious. Several boats pass in the creek, slowing down, and I nonverbally signal "hello," "feel free to speed up and pass" and "thanks." We hug the edge of the marsh to stay out of the incoming tide from Five Fathom Creek and then make the wide turn to the north, flowing with Five Fathom

Creek's incoming movement. There is windward work ahead in this passage through Clubhouse Creek. It is cool, and I am layered with a T-shirt, a long underwear top, a raingear jacket, sweatpants, neoprene socks and sandals.

More people are heading out on the water, and the breeze, as predicted, is rising. The passage is marked by bird events: two wood storks headed for the mainland and a flight of two-dozen egrets over the marsh to the south. Once out into Muddy Bay, we retrace the southward course of *Island Cat* that I made in April on my first visit to Lighthouse Island, my destination today. The course will take us into a creek connecting with the Romain River and then Lighthouse Island. It is a fine, broad reach across the bay, allowing for good speed and hastened by the tide change from flow to ebb. Scattered boats fish around Muddy Bay, a large, shallow body of water of presently expanded dimensions due to the high tide. A view to the southwest reveals another shallow body of water: Oyster Bay. We finally find the wide mouth of the creek to the south—our portal to the Romain River. The breeze has picked up, and the bend to the east in the creek now has us on a beam reach. Anticipating spray, it is time to shed the sweatpants for a bathing suit on this warm day. A cormorant is beating out toward Muddy Bay, and a pelican soars high. Soon, this bird has reduced altitude to glide two mast lengths directly above me, and it cranes its neck downward as I stretch mine to gaze upward for this encounter.

Progress is rapid, and before long we're at the junction of this creek and Romain River known as the Crossroads. This sizable creek has no name on the chart; it flows out into Key Inlet. It is smoother water at this point of sail between a close reach and closehauled, and the lighthouses are getting closer. There is plenty of water at this stage of tide. A johnboat is fishing off the clam structure by Mill Island. Cape Island is straight ahead, but to starboard a small creek enters the marsh toward the northwest end of Lighthouse Island. Toward the midpoint of the island, some posts of an old dock mark the old landing. This is our spot, so I round up into the wind, drop sail and turn to coast with the wind into this landing, now silted in and populated by *Spartina* and oysters. I step out into the cordgrass and secure *Kingfisher* with bow and stern lines to old piling stubs. I keep her out in the water, hoping that with the falling tide I won't have too tough of a time floating her later.

I grab my gear from *Kingfisher* and walk on the narrow path through the vegetation run riot to the lighthouses. The objective today is a walk around Lighthouse Island. After a return to the craft to retrieve my forgotten hiking stick, I walk to the larger of the two lighthouses and stop on the smooth concrete pad to change into clothes for a hike, including long sleeves and shoes. A side trip over to the older lighthouse includes a look inside, and I note a goat skeleton on the dirt floor. Nearby, there are stands of chinaberry trees with their distinctive yellow fruit. I noticed their appearance here on my trip in April, and they appear to be an artifact of the lightkeepers who set up homesteads here in the nineteenth century. The scouting for trails from here is not fruitful. The vegetation seems impenetrable, even for bushwhacking, so I look over toward the southeast in the direction of a stand of pines.

I step into a little open area, and some elevation change indicates the presence of old dunes. But there is no trail, and soon the walk bogs down in thickets of vines, dominated by dune greenbrier and poison ivy. Heading to the more open sandy areas seems logical, yet here the way is guarded by a covering of dune devil-joints, or dune prickly-pear, armed with one- to two-inch spikes. Soon I am not just picking my way through but also picking off a coating of these jagged hitchhikers from my shoes and pants. The good news is there are only a few lingering mosquitoes today.

The path truly requires bushwhacking as I attempt to cut across this end of the island to reach the marsh. Finally making it to the pines, I find that the way is still difficult, with continued vine thickets. A heavy mat of pine straw covers the vine-laced earth, and I use my hiking stick to probe ahead. I have worked up a sweat, so entering into an open area after this section of pines allows the relief of the solid northeast breeze. Another forested area dominated by cedars appears ahead, but there are many false trails ending in an impenetrable thicket. Some effort brings me to another area of pines. A startling loud animal noise occurs ahead, and I initially wonder if it might be a vagrant goat that avoided removal from the island several years ago. The noise comes from a tree and is, in fact, a great blue heron, which leaves its perch with a squawk as I approach. There is still no good trail, and following wildlife paths doesn't help much. Backtracking some, I head more to the south along the edge of old dunes and finally find more open areas and the accompanying dune devil-joints. More groves of cedars precede the final thicket of wax myrtle, yaupon and sea myrtle before the marsh. This is a solid hedgerow with no openings, so picking the best place, I battle through to the other side.

A different world emerges, with a large section of marsh between the edge of Lighthouse Island and what was known as South Cape Island to the south. The edge of the island thicket and marsh will be my path to walk around the island. I head to the west, walking the ecotone between *Spartina* and sea ox-eyes. The water is a couple inches deep in the marsh flat. Marsh lavender blooms purple in this boundary between two different botanical worlds. The island bends to the north, and the spine I noticed on the satellite image sticks out from the marsh ahead, though separated from where I stand by a shallow creek. I decide to stick to the main island and continue around the bend. At this moment, a flock of tree swallows comes in from the marsh toward the island—hundreds and hundreds of these darting flyers. It is one of those glorious moments I am most grateful to observe. The quietness amplifies the sounds of the birds wheeling and turning. The large marsh flat between Lighthouse Island and the jutting spine to the south presents a view all the way to the houses along the ICW in McClellanville. The swallows continue to flow to the island and gather in the pine trees.

The long, narrow hammock to the southwest beckons, but that walk will have to wait for another day. I continue the walk along this side of Lighthouse Island between the edge of the marsh and the high ground, here encountering a carpet of glassworts. The mud is the color of milk chocolate. The expanse of the marsh flat is immense. A great egret appears ahead in the marsh, and raccoon trails disperse through the grass. Ahead on the edge of marsh and high ground is a brick structure. It initially suggests an oyster pit, but on closer inspection, the presence of a ceramic drain pipe running through horizontally seems to be a drain for the former lightkeepers' residences. Farther along, piles of a former dock appear on the point, and a kingfisher circling and crying out marks his territory. The point is defined by a small creek through the marsh with a three-foot bank, with enough depth and width to float a canoe. It is no longer an easy walk, and more obstacles appear ahead. I'm not sure if it is walkable on the other side, so it is time to turn and retrace my steps.

Once back at the small creek separating Lighthouse Island from the hammock spine to the southwest, there is a view toward Key Inlet, and visible are the cabin sides of an anchored yacht in the small bay there. I continue retracing my steps past the place where I came out of the island's interior. The slope becomes steeper along the edge toward the east end of the island, with thickets of goldenrod, wax myrtle, yaupon, sea myrtle and

Lighthouse Island

Lighthouses over the marsh on Lighthouse Island.

a few palmettos. A clapper rail starts ahead from the marsh, the second one I've seen today. At the east end, there are fine views of the barrier island in front, the inlet and Cape Island. Once around the point, the views are of Cape Romain Harbor and Mill Island. A nice bleached pine log presents itself at the high tide line as a pleasant stopping point for lunch and the enjoyment of these views.

After lunch, another clapper rail is spooked by my footsteps approaching the landing. A northern harrier patrols over the tops of the trees, veering back and forth and reaching fast across the northeast breeze. It is reassuring to see the mast of *Kingfisher*; no other craft has joined her at the landing. The return plan is to leave before low tide, catch the last of the outgoing tide, heading west in the Romain River and Santee Path Creek, and then take the preliminary incoming tide in Five Fathom Creek back to Jeremy Creek. Retrieving the gear from the base of the lighthouse, I note the fine view to the harbor and reflect on having this island and its place in this wilderness area all to myself.

Not ready to leave the island yet, I leave the extra gear at the landing and continue the walk to the west on this side of the island along the marsh edge. Making it to the point, I recognize some familiar landmarks and realize that I have made a complete circuit of the island as I view the dock piles within thirty yards. A fence stands on this point, composed more of solid ground than marsh. The narrow creek winds close by, still holding water within two hours of low tide. The high bank is nearly vertical, except where the creek turns forty-five degrees. This could be a potential landing site for *Kingfisher*.

I must get underway while there is still water left in the Romain River. I pack up the gear so it can be stowed in *Kingfisher* quickly and haul the craft to where she can float. I have drastically underestimated the tidal drop—I am twenty feet from water. A sizable oyster bank lies straight out from the piles. Contemplating this mess, I use the bow mooring line still tethered to the mast as a hauling line. At least it is a little downhill; with each haul, we make about five feet. When getting into the shell area, I direct *Kingfisher* through the *Spartina* to help "grease the skids." We are finally to water, with a hard base of oyster shells underfoot. The course will be off to the west, so I must walk the craft out into deeper water before hoisting sail. The firm bottom is now gone, and I am in soft mud. With no luck finding firmer footing, and from a somewhat sunken position, I raise sail as best as possible. In rapid succession it is down rudder, down daggerboard (partially) and in sail, with half of my body in the boat and my muddy shoes dragging behind. It is a most awkward sailing position, but I make it off the lee shore covered with extensive oyster banks and swing my feet onto the foredeck to take off the muddy shoes.

Tying the muddy footwear to the splash rail is just the first duty required in putting *Kingfisher* in sailing shape, as the mooring line is flopped on a mud-spattered deck, numerous gear bags are loose in the cockpit and I'm wet up to the waist. The winds have moderated, and it has warmed up, so the wetness is no problem. The course is west in the Romain River, and the objective is to get west quickly before being swallowed up by the rapidly shoaling water as in my earlier trip to Mill Island in April. The course back to Jeremy Creek will be via Romain River, Santee Path Creek and Five Fathom Creek.

We sail down the Romain River, outrunning the shoaling water, and occasionally pass boats fishing and running by. Some outgoing tide still flows out Key Inlet, and once in the mouth of Santee Path Creek, we run with the last of this outgoing tide. The breeze has dropped further, and the sail through the creek is with limited sound. The exhalation of dolphins punctuates the creek's serenity. They dive under *Kingfisher*, and the water disturbance swirls around the hull, but they only reappear when well clear. I wonder if they recognize individual craft by the sound of motors or perhaps even by sonic profile. A shrimp skips across the water close by. A squawk ahead reveals the presence of a harrier now flying over the marsh on patrol. The creek has reached low tide, and the wind is on the starboard aft quarter. The sky is still mainly clear, with a couple of small clouds to the west. The easy sailing allows for recalling blackbirds in the *Spartina* in March and processing the adventure on Lighthouse Island today. The timing seems right for not reaching Five Fathom Creek before the tide change.

The breeze is dying in concert with the end of the outgoing tide. *Kingfisher* is sitting without wind for a while, but ahead the old wooden creek marker signals the entrance to Five Fathom Creek. The wind is now light and in the nose; a pair of dolphins ahead spy me and dive assertively, rising astern. We are finally out in Five Fathom, and the wind is all over the compass. There is a little wind from the southwest now, and there are many more clouds off to the west. No-see-ums are present in these drifting conditions. A billow of smoke to the southwest on the mainland goes straight up—not a good sign. There is another gasp of breathing astern—a long gulp. The stillness allows me to hear and then see the adult loggerhead for several seconds before the dive. The boom is going back and forth in the variable wind; the conditions reinforce my decision to return before low tide rather than waiting until after the turn.

A trawler seen across the marsh in the distance is coming into the creek. A little wind returns from the northeast, and I hug the east side of the creek to make way for the small craft. It steams by before we reach the point with the bend to the northeast. A large offshore sport fisherman cruises by kicking up a swell breaking on the shore, which I hug, generating the wave from the cordgrass. Looking for the wind, *Kingfisher* is hit by a blast that starts the sheet out with the sail shaking hard, and my hat blows off and lands on the aft deck. My relief at the wind's return is short-lived as it drops off again, and I wonder why the wind gods did not read the marine forecast: ten to fifteen knots from the northeast this afternoon! But soon the returned breeze allows for sheeting in with nice sailing to windward. Having wind is appreciated as more craft are coming through this waterway, and a larger trawler is also headed our way from the bay.

Further wind variation has the wind at southeast, so the point of sail is a reach. I pass three kayakers, who mention their visit to the Georgetown Wooden Boat Show earlier today. I give them a heads-up about the approaching trawler. I make the turn into Town Creek and recall past musings about sharing this narrow waterway with a large trawler, now to become a reality. I hug the east side and search for the bottom with my daggerboard until I touch, pulling up the board some and maintaining the proximity with the shore. The trawler swings in around a bend, and the variable wind now has the sail full as he passes. He throttled down earlier, and his passing reveals the name on the stern, *Miss Candace*. A johnboat follows closely in his wake.

Entering the last narrow section of this creek before the ICW, the wind veers to the north, requiring beating, and this becomes an issue as another trawler appears astern. I take again to hugging the east side, barely maintaining my course closehauled. As the small trawler, *Miss Sandra II*, nears, I can no longer lay the shore, and with a tack out of the question, I grab my paddle and take a few easy strokes to maintain my heading. The trawler is by and I relax. We tack to enter the ICW, and I decide to cross the ICW to stay clear of the traffic. I continue to use the paddle as an auxiliary in the light wind. The traffic coming into Jeremy Creek includes a yacht looking for an overnight berth and another small trawler. Staying clear of this busy channel, I drop sail for the final coast in.

The Georgetown guide and his party dock just after me. I get my trailer and back down the ramp, while the guide heads off to get his truck and trailer. His party tells me that they wondered about me when the wind died. I mention the value of the incoming tide. They did not have a good day fishing, and the guide is clearly disappointed. I pull out *Kingfisher* and, due to the traffic at the landing, pull into another space to unrig and prepare for the ride home. Another fisherman pulls out; he mentions seeing me and wonders what my course was. I relate the path of my sail and ask about his catch. It was also not good, but he feels better when he hears that the Georgetown guide did not do well either. Saying goodbye, he heads for his short pull home in the village, and I head south to Awendaw.

Lighthouse Island

November 6, 2006

Low tide 2:00 p.m. Predicted winds NE 20–25 knots.

The Ashley Landing is cold this morning and accentuated by a very high tide. My van never leaves the horizontal as I back *Kingfisher* to the water. A big raft of gulls floats right by the ramp, and only a half dozen trucks and trailers are at the landing on this brisk, windy morning. A couple of snowbirds are heading out of the marina up the creek as I prepare to sail, suited up in layers, rain gear and wet suit socks, prepared to get wet. I am easily off and out at 8:30 a.m., along with an outboard carrying a passenger wearing a woolen face mask. A tug and snowbird ahead in the ICW are steering south. This time of year the ICW is a major thoroughfare, and as we come into this waterway, a sailboat off to port, carrying a headsail, is also heading south. We leave this traffic behind as our angled course takes us into Town Creek to join with Five Fathom Creek.

The wind is from behind, and so we're running with an outgoing tide and the promise of an increasing wind. I reflect on my earlier thoughts to abandon the planned sail due to the forecast of twenty to twenty-five knots, but as I suspected, the conditions are more moderate inshore. It is easy sailing now, with no traffic in Five Fathom Creek. The increase in the tide's ebb is evident on the sail out, and as I move farther away from the ICW, I can see the mast and sail of the snowbird seen earlier plowing south in the ditch. Progress for *Kingfisher* is swift, and we make the entrance to the Santee Path Creek in just over thirty minutes. The course we will take today to Lighthouse Island is different from my previous trip two weeks ago. Today's course recreates the most likely course of the Lighthouse Service personnel on their regular trip from McClellanville to Lighthouse Island, both in the days of oars and sail and in the modern era of internal combustion engines.

We begin the sail through this passage high in the marsh due to the height of the tide. I had anticipated a course without tacks—a close reach or closehauled course. There are bends to the northeast that require going to windward, and the strong ebb is opposing us. I recall my battle on a similar course in Papas Creek in September, though fortunately there is more wind today. Yet it is still a significant battle, and I waste no time since the tide's quickening will make matters worse. After over half an hour of battling upwind and against the tide, we encounter a creek on the north side of the marsh before a large bend back to the east. This creek is emptying much water out into this waterway, and a tongue of water grabs *Kingfisher* and gives a significant push to leeward before letting go. But now the battle is over, since the flow is neutral at this point and perhaps positive in the course to the east. The view up the creek ahead includes the lighthouse in the distance and signals my connection with Nellie Creek and Romain River. And with the turn into this waterway to the south, we are off, with the advantage of wind and time in our favor.

With the turn to the east in Romain River, we are sailing to windward again, but with the outgoing tide, the progress is good. The waterway becomes more open, and the conditions create some chop. The water becomes more disturbed at the intersection of other waterways, and the first dolphin sightings occur at these junctions. We are past the waterway angling back to the southwest that leads to Raccoon and Key Creeks. The proximity to the Crossroads, the junction of the Romain River with the large creek leading out to Key Inlet, invites contemplation of my landing spot for accessing the part of Lighthouse Island I seek today: the long narrow spine stretching away from the main island to the west-northwest. The satellite image alerted me initially to this elevated ridge in the marsh, and my trip the previous month inspired this second visit. The satellite image also showed a creek paralleling this spine and penetrating in from Key Inlet. The day before, I had asked Gene Morrison about this creek and wondered if I might be able to access the high ground along here. He recalled being in this creek this summer but wasn't sure about accessing the high ground without doing it at high tide and walking through the marsh. My other course would be to sail to the northwest point of the main island and make a landing by accessing the little creek I found two weeks ago.

Reaching the Crossroads, I bear off to head into Key Inlet, but after fifty yards of sailing off on a strong wind, I abort this plan and head up, playing an eddy along the eastern side of this creek to beat back up to the Romain River. My decision allows me to keep my windward gauge and maintain the east heading in Romain River. We are now opposed to some outgoing flow, but without any deep channels the water movement is relatively slow. There is some chop, and once again tacks are required in this course to windward. We encounter a small section of disturbed water on the south side of this waterway, caused by a creek discharging

Lighthouse Island

water from the extensive marsh here. Across from Mill Island and almost to Lighthouse Island's northwest point, I search for the tiny creek for access to the land, staying close to the south side. I see the point, and the fence at the place where I will land, but no entrance to the creek is evident. I tack and backtrack, searching again for the opening, but find nothing. I am perplexed, and the conditions are rougher now, with the predicted stronger wind. Should I run back to Key Inlet and search beyond my previous aborted attempt? I am losing time on my planned walk, so I elect to take another close look along the marsh. This time, I see a tiny waterway heading in at a forty-five-degree angle through the cordgrass, indicated by the water flowing out. Without any further deliberation, I round up, drop the sail—much of it in the water—and turn *Kingfisher* to enter the marsh. Coming in perpendicular to the marsh edge, the daggerboard hits oysters, so it is up with the board and into the boat. I have to paddle to make the turn into the creek, and now we are in high *Spartina*.

Water is flowing out, so vigorous paddling is required, and the popping off and sinking of the protective cap on the paddle handle is not a good sign.

Kingfisher in a creek on Lighthouse Island, with Cape Island in distant background.

This tiny, hidden creek has a few turns, and soon we are into a small opening in the marsh. After a bend, we continue through this tiny creek until we enter the nice basin I found two weeks ago, with the high ground and bank and the fence close by. A post makes a suitable mooring spot. After landing, I grab the needed gear and scramble up the muddy bank, changing shoes and loading my pack with food and drink. I pick my way across this point, through wetlands and cedar thicket, to the western side of Lighthouse Island for the walk south to explore the elevated spine.

This is a walk I am retracing from two weeks before, but the water is higher, so at times I am slogging through one-inch to ankle-deep water. At the crossing to the spine to the west, I encounter water deeper than anticipated. Pulling up my pants over my knees still may not keep the clothes dry. With no desire to wade across waist-level water, I select a different direction for the crossing, hoping I won't stumble into soft mud. Once across, I decide to walk the south side of this long hammock first. There is a lot of water here, and I alternate between slogging through water up to the ankles and sea ox-eyes up to the waist. It gets easier ahead with a shallower slope. The satellite image had revealed that beside this spine another narrow spine connected at its end and reached back to the southeast, essentially creating a wishbone shape. At some point on the walk, I enter into the wishbone and find myself looking across at the other side. The hammock I am walking next to is a thicket of wax myrtle, sea myrtle, cedar and yaupon holly with red berries. There is also *Spartina patens* along this edge in places.

An unnatural object sits above the high-tide line. It is an approximately fifteen-foot-long torpedo-like object, pointed on each end and appearing to be made out of aluminum. Its apparent distance from the water suggests that it arrived here by a storm tide, most likely courtesy of Hurricane Hugo in 1989. Torpedo or nuclear weapon initially comes to mind. I photograph it, and later Gene Morrison suggests that it is a paravane, even before he sees the photo. A paravane is a device towed behind minesweepers, U.S. Navy ships in the twentieth century that operated out of the now closed Charleston Naval Base. Gene related that derelict paravanes were occasionally found in these waters and used by enterprising individuals as pontoons for rafts.

The hammock is a solid thicket without openings or places to walk. I am still walking in water, but it feels good. It has warmed up for my walk; since I am both in the sun and in the lee of the hammock, I shed my beanie and fleece layer. I am in the middle of the wishbone, and there is a marsh flat extending to the other side. At the end of this hammock, there is a shallow creek creating a separation from the next hammock, which from this vantage point has its own profile, much like a fishhook. I have reached my turnaround time and head back east on the northern side of the hammock. I am motivated to make time: I must get out of the creek and the Romain River before I am locked in by low tide and then catch the last of the outgoing tide in Santee Path Creek before Five Fathom Creek. It is an easier walk here, and there is a carpet of glassworts in red fall color. I feel again the brisk northeast wind. The marsh is expansive, stretching out to the Romain River, though due to the flatness of the landscape, this waterway is not visible.

I consider a shortcut across the marsh flat to the main body of Lighthouse Island but realize there are creeks that would be difficult to cross. From this perspective, the older of the two lighthouses is half the height of the other. The hammock to the right is extensively populated with cedars. All of this land was once part of the Raccoon Key, or Keys, as labeled on several of the old maps. On approaching the crossing of the creek ahead, a little shortcut across the flat leads to shallower water than at the previously made crossing. No lingering here—haste is needed, though I make one stop to photograph feeding willets. I cut across the small thicket at the point, following animal trails for the easiest route. The first view of the basin holding *Kingfisher* is startling due to the significantly dropped water level; the creek running upstream from the basin is completely dry, exposing oyster clusters. With some frenzy, I pack the gear, undo the mooring line and throw everything in *Kingfisher*. Once down the bank, it is clear that the propulsion will not be via paddling but by pulling the boat through the creek. In places it is only inches deep, and I must pull the hull across the mud and shells; fortunately, the mud is firm underfoot. Prior to a pool of water, the oysters become thick, requiring me to clear them out of the path of the dragged hull, the mud just barely lubricated with the fallen water. It is a luxury in the pool to float and paddle across before reaching the last section of creek and the return of the dragging effort. When I reach the proximity of the creek mouth at the Romain River, the firm bottom morphs into soft pluff mud and the oysters become thick, with solid oyster rock on each side of the tiny opening to the waterway.

It will be a real challenge making sail out of here. The island and this so-called river seem to have a grip on *Kingfisher*. The strong northeast breeze is blowing directly onto this bank of the Romain River, growing shallower by the minute, effectively pinning me here. I begin to paddle off of this lee shore before raising sail and setting off. This is easier said than done. Sitting on the bow and paddling out as hard as possible, I achieve limited progress. We are fighting both the wind and chop; some waves are coming over the bow, and keeping the bow into the wind is difficult. Despite pulling hard, we are now at a standstill about twenty feet off the bank, with the grip of the island strong. I desire to stay out of the water and plan to push the daggerboard into the soft mud as sort of an anchor prior to raising sail. The first attempt to do so is foiled with a line in the daggerboard trunk preventing the board going down, and ten feet are quickly lost. Finally, the board is down and we are stopped, but the angle of the craft to the wind is not optimal for raising sail. Despite the awkward position, I raise the sail up, cleat the halyard off and prepare to sail off this lee shore.

The rudder is down, but multiple efforts to bring the bow around to head off on the starboard tack by backing the sail don't work. Hindsight later informed me that the board "anchoring" the craft did not allow the heading to change. The breeze is strong, and in the hubbub I miss the paddle being washed off the bow. I notice it now, floating toward the lee shore and oyster rock off to port. It is an instant where getting off immediately and bearing off on a reach for a quick grab of the paddle might save it, but the moment is quickly gone. To get it now would require dropping sail and walking the boat across the mud and oyster-strewn bank. I dismiss this option, prioritizing getting off and out before the outgoing tide swallows me up, and let the paddle go.

In the midst of this chaos, a johnboat with two young men I saw earlier comes roaring up, with outboard tilted to navigate the shallow waters, obviously seeing my current struggle. Across the wind, two statements pass: "Sir, there is no water in here" and "My paddle has floated off." They offer to lend me their paddle, but their efforts to get close are hindered by the shallow water. Somewhere in this interaction I hear, "Your sail is muddy" from the grinning passenger. The johnboat operator takes a try at recovering my paddle but without success. Taking a new tack—literally—I sheet in on the present angle, and with *Kingfisher* on the port tack, I pull up the daggerboard a little and fight to claw off and not be washed back onto the bank. Some headway is the first sign of victory. When out to the middle of the waterway, I come around, now on the starboard tack and heading west on the course out of this rapidly shoaling waterway. Passing the duo in the johnboat, I give them the thumbs up as I head off on a broad reach.

The water is definitely shallow, and even with the daggerboard up it still hits, at times with the rudder also kicking up some. A new problem is more troublesome, however: the joint between the two spars holding the sail (boom and upper boom) has come apart, and my last repair of this eaten-away aluminum connection has failed. I anticipated this problem and carried extra tools today for this possibility. There is no way to pull out the tools here, however, and slowing to do so would certainly ground us until released by the incoming tide several hours later. It is holding together somewhat but looks like it could completely detach, and with the released force applied to the repaired sail, a major tear could result. Without the vang applied, the pressures on this joint appear rough on this broad reach, so in a little open area I round up and set some vang. It appears to make things a bit better, but damage is possible without some more attention. But we're racing both with and against the outgoing tide. Still finding shoals that kick up the rudder, and recalling Gene Morrison mentioning a little more water on the south side of the Romain River before the Crossroads, I steer toward this area.

Once past the Crossroads, and relieved at getting out of the shoaling waterway, I take the opportunity to run up on a mudflat, "anchor" *Kingfisher* with the daggerboard shoved down into the mud and make a jury rig with a spare piece of line, lashing the tack to the boom with a reef knot. It is then up with the board, push off and continue sailing west. Another set of old reading glasses are sacrificed to the creek, a mishap typical of the mess on *Kingfisher*. We are now running through the Santee Path Creek and relaxing while eating lunch in the starkly calm conditions. At times, the relative calm creates a too-casual approach that almost puts us up on the creek bank. Several jibes are required through here, and I watch the rig carefully to see how it handles these jolts. Another johnboat passes and is the only other craft I see in this creek. Before the junction with Five Fathom Creek, we find a creek on the north side to round up into. With the words, "Your sail is muddy" lingering, I drop sail and apply a wet sponge to effect a more tidy appearance of *Kingfisher* before the passage to Jeremy Creek.

In Five Fathom Creek we round up to a close reach and, without traffic, begin the next leg of the homeward passage. The tide has changed to incoming, and the timing for the switch is perfect as it helps propel us home. The wind is ten to fifteen knots, and the smooth water makes the sailing good. Pelicans and cormorants cluster on one bank, and cormorants are sentinels on channel markers. We pass only a boat or two in the whole length of the passage into Town Creek. Once again, the easy sailing has me in a trance, and a puff heels *Kingfisher* way over before I restore balance. The creek is wide, but we run aground. Coming through Town Creek, the sound of a piece of metal echoes off the forward deck, and a stainless s-hook lies there for retrieval, having fallen out of the jury-rigged sail tack and spar junction. While trying to squeeze by a shell rake at the entrance to the ICW, the daggerboard hits the hard shell with a crunch. Crossing the ICW, an obstacle in the guise of an eddy opposes *Kingfisher* near the southwest point at the entrance to Jeremy Creek. A workboat is ahead and pulls in at the floating dock at the landing. We wait for the fisherman to haul his craft out before our landing to cap off this latest Lighthouse Island adventure.

CAPE ISLAND

The barrier and marsh islands of the Cape Romain National Wildlife Refuge northeast of Bull Island bulge out miles into the Atlantic Ocean, with the farthest prominence located on Cape Island. Like other capes along the Carolina coast, the bulge of sand continues underwater in a tongue stretching out several miles, capped with the shallow waters of the Cape Romain Shoals. A number of vessels pushed by stormy weather have found the coast on these shoals, while other vessels ended up directly on the sandy strand. The exposure of Cape Island to the ocean forces has made it a precarious and unstable platform, constantly on the move and morphing into new shapes.

Cape Romain is the southernmost of the four capes along the mid-Atlantic coast identified as cuspate forelands; the other three are Capes Hatteras, Lookout and Fear. These cuspate forelands are projections out from the shoreline in a triangular shape, either perpendicular to or at an angle to the coast's line. Though different theories have been proposed for their existence, the most plausible suggests that they are the result of a geographic area with two predominate and opposite wind directions. Cape Romain is certainly a function of the northeast and southwest winds prevalent at different times of the year. The North Carolina capes are noted to erode on the northern flank and accrete on the western flank. This model does not fit Cape Romain, since both flanks are relatively symmetrical. There is also an anomaly with a longshore sediment current moving to the north. The north end of Cape Island has been growing in that direction for perhaps the last

Cape Island
June 10, 2006
September 3, 2006

N

Murphy Island

Alligator Creek

Ramhorn Cr

Mill Cr

Casino Creek

Cape Romain Harbor

Cape Island

Congaree Boat Creek

Horsehead Creek

Joe & Ben Cr

Mill Island

Slack Reach

Devils Den

Romain River

Lighthouse Island

McClellanville

Intracoastal Waterway

Dabe Creek

Stripe Creek

Jeremy Island

Clubhouse Creek

Muddy Bay

Raccoon Creek

Key Inlet

Jeremy Creek

Little Papas Creek

Papas Creek

Nellie Creek

Santee Path Creek

Key Creek

Raccoon Key

Five Fathom Creek

Long Creek

Sett Creek

Bull River

White Banks

Sandy Point

Miles

two hundred years. This is probably the only place in South Carolina where

84

there is this northern longshore current. Miles Hayes and Jacqueline Michel have speculated that this difference is a result of the sheltering of Cape from the dominant northeast winds by the mass of the Santee Delta. Additionally, the landward movement of these barrier islands has increased the protection afforded by the delta.

From far overhead, above the altitude of seabirds, the island's profile resembles a shark—the snout pointing toward Murphy Island, the dorsal fin shaped by Cowpen Point jutting out to the northwest and the tail fin uncharacteristically rounded, reflecting the rounded shape of Mill Island to the northwest. At an opposite pole to its sister barrier, Bull Island, to the southeast, the islands also are diametrically opposed in their structure. Bull is a prograding and Cape is a transgressive barrier island. The rise in sea level is keeping Cape Island moving at a rapid clip. Its migration is seen readily in the development of the backside of the island by extensive overwash, a phenomenon seen all along the strand. One of the other processes allowing barriers to grow landward is the welding of flood-tide deltas onto the barrier. The rounded "tail fin" of Cape is the result of the incorporation of a flood-tide delta formed by an inlet here in the past. The narrowness of Cape Island is a reason for its ability to respond to the rapid movement required to keep up with the rise in sea level. Islands like Cape are known, besides the technical description of "transgressive," as thin, retreating barriers. And rapid the movement has been, with the rate of travel measured on an average of twenty feet per year for the years 1941 to 1973. The rate has been observed to increase thereafter, with Hurricane Hugo accelerating the retreat.

The beaches of Cape Romain have the distinction of being the most erosional on the South Carolina coast. The main reason behind this fact is the lack of sediment available. This lack is definitely a reduction from previous supplies and is, in part, the result of the damming of the Santee River and the resulting choking off of sediment flow out of the river's mouth to the north.

While the ongoing processes of surf and currents continue the transformation of this island, major storms are the real movers and shakers. Hurricane Hugo completely inundated all of the islands of the cape. Cape Island was flattened, with the destruction of trees and the scraping of the ten-foot dunes to a much lower profile. Hugo not only increased the landward movement but also blew out sections of the narrow barriers, with the biggest

Cape Island
June 10, 2006   ....»
September 3, 2006 ----►

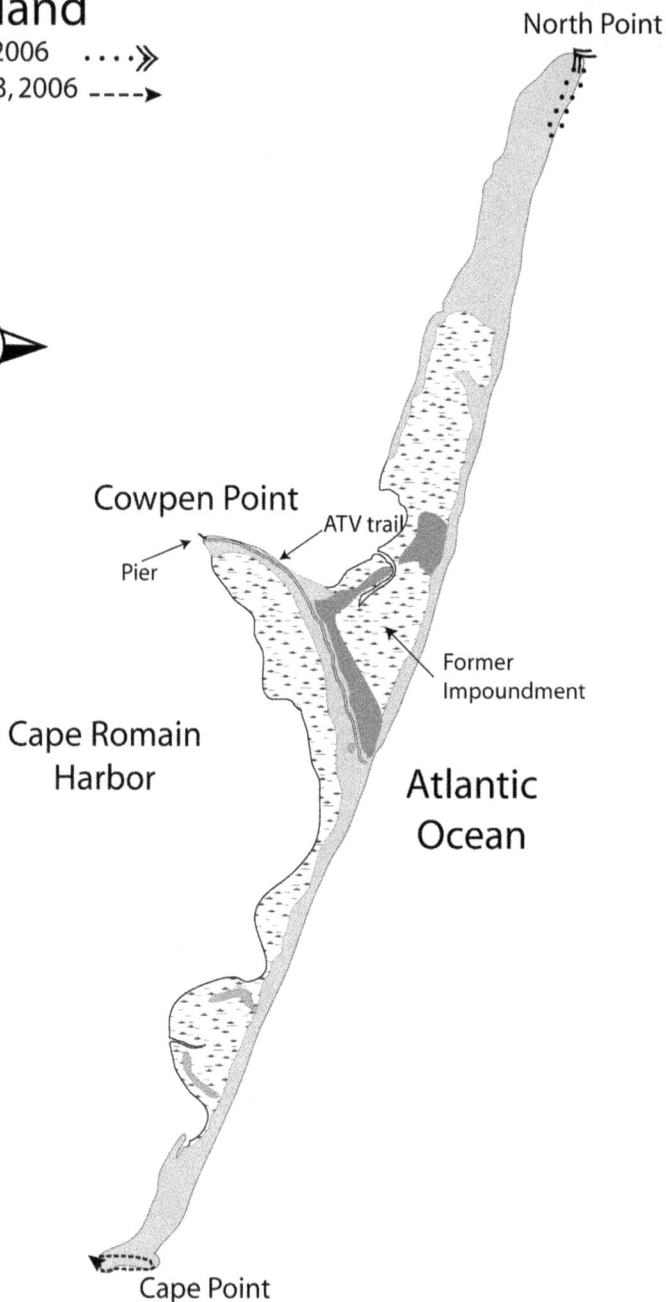

North Point

N

Cowpen Point

ATV trail

Pier

Former
Impoundment

Cape Romain
Harbor

Atlantic
Ocean

Cape Point

0   1/2   1   2

Miles

breach in the center of Cape Island. It originally was almost twelve hundred yards wide but narrowed into a small tidal inlet. It finally closed to make the strand once again connected. The island was divided again in 1996 by the passing of Hurricane Bertha along the coast. The old, historical inlet by the southern tip of Cape Island was reopened and has remained open to this day. So the island, previously with the shape of a backward *L*, was separated close to the Cape's point.

The island has a number of interesting features. A small ridge located in the central part of the island angles off the beach strand to the northwest, providing the structure for Cowpen Point. This is an old re-curved spit at this end of the island. On the 1854 chart, Cape Island has a point protruding to the northwest that corresponds with Cowpen Point. Currently, the island has another point to the east of Cowpen that follows the island's eastern profile to the north. This is a new re-curved spit that is continuing to accrete toward Murphy Island. Cowpen Point and an area stretching toward the beach are the location of a dune field botanical community, much larger than anywhere else in the refuge. The northern end of the island is also populated by a large dune field. As this point has accreted north toward Murphy Island, the dune field botanical community has stabilized the sands.

Between Cowpen Point and the beach is located a grove of pine trees. The rise in elevation from Cowpen Point toward the beach in the center of the island allows for the development of this maritime forest, mainly characterized by loblolly pines. John DuPre, son of Andrew "Binks" DuPre, says that during his father's time as refuge manager, he planted pines on the island.

Cape Island was the location for the creation of an impoundment in the 1930s at the same time as Jacks Creek was built on Bull Island. The plan was to make a three-hundred-acre waterfowl marsh, mainly flooded with fresh water. The Romain WPA Camp was set up on the island to provide on-site "housing" for the workers. As part of the reconditioning of the island, the project also included the planting of short leaf pines, American hollies, cabbage palmettos and myrtles. The dike built as the third side of the Cape Island impoundment is still standing in a straight line toward the northeast, though it is now breached with a creek into the marsh that allows fishermen access from Cape Romain Harbor. For a number of years, there was also a wading bird rookery located here. This pond has long ago been breached from the ocean side, losing considerable area from erosion, and overall is much changed from its original form.

This island became a landmark for mariners in the years before the installation of lighthouses along this coast. In fact, the Spanish riding the Gulf Stream up the coast would use the cape as their jumping-off point to head east on their return voyages across the Atlantic. The English named this prominence Cape Carteret, and early charts display this label. This island, and the Cape Romain Shoals a couple miles off the cape, has also been the tragic end for a number of ships over the years. Though North Carolina is better known for shipwrecks, with its Graveyard of the Atlantic, this section of the coast has had its share. Similar to the wrecking ground to the north, south-bearing ships would often hug the coast to stay inside of the effects of the northern-flowing Gulf Stream, and errors in navigation or stormy weather would lead the vessels into shallow waters. Due to the isolation of this sandy island, often the only assistance available for wrecked ships came from passing vessels.

Cape Island has been the destination for the annual nesting of a large number of loggerhead turtles (*Caretta caretta*). The nesting colony for loggerheads on Cape Island is the most significant on the East Coast north of Florida. Besides the turtle's choice of this site, a number of factors combine to support the conservation of loggerheads on Cape Island: distance from the mainland and man-made light sources, the protection from future development via its location in the Cape Romain National Wildlife Refuge and the designation of this section of the refuge as a Class I Wilderness Area. Another factor contributes to the importance of this nesting colony. The temperature of the sand impacts sexual differences in embryos in the nest: cooler temperatures produce more males. With the Florida colonies generating more females, Cape Island produces an important share of males.

In the summer of 1939, two employees of Cape Romain National Wildlife Refuge studied the loggerhead nesting extensively and wrote a report titled "The Loggerheads of Cape Romain." William Baldwin Jr., father of author William Baldwin, and John M. Lofton Jr. lived on the island for the loggerhead nesting season from May through September. The conditions were primitive, and they were without the tools used by twenty-first-century staff, such as powerful outboards and all-terrain vehicles (ATVs) towing trailers for gear and people. Instead, Baldwin and Lofton

Cape Island

had an oyster bateau with a five-horsepower engine at their disposal and got around the island on foot. They asked a number of questions in their work and collected and analyzed data. They noted that the population of loggerheads had declined from several decades previous. In 1939, their count of nests was the following: Cape Island, four hundred nests; Raccoon Key, two hundred nests; and Bull Island, thirty nests. Historical information included the existence of a turtle "industry" in the past on Cape Island. In a single night, collectors took seven hundred dozen eggs. Some impatient egg collectors would not wait for the crawling turtles to lay their eggs but would cut them open for egg removal and leave the dying turtles on the beach.

Currently, a management program to benefit the loggerhead turtles is conducted annually by the USFWS. The Cape Island sea turtle nesting project has been headed up since 1989 by Sarah Dawsey, wildlife biologist of Cape Romain National Wildlife Refuge. The project utilizes volunteer help extensively: in 2006, more than thirty-two hundred hours of volunteer labor were collectively performed by over fifty volunteers. Dawsey has recruited a loyal cadre of volunteers and continues each year the recruitment of potential volunteers prepared to make the commitment and meet the challenging conditions often encountered by Cape Island. In 2005, I offered my services in the building of the hatcheries on the island. As required, I attended a volunteer information meeting at the Sewee Center in April 2005, with Sarah Dawsey giving the presentation about the volunteer program. Her talk promised the following on the island: black widow spiders, water moccasins, biting gnats, mosquitoes, greenhead flies, deer flies, sharks patrolling the beach and thunderstorms during which volunteers would be required to lay down in low spots in the dunes. Though I would not be able to make the commitment to make the trip once a week for the daily conservation work, three days for building the hatcheries was doable, and Dawsey's advertisement of the conditions was strangely attractive.

The loggerhead management program includes full-time employees, seasonal employees, interns and the volunteer corps, but clearly the leadership, heart and soul of the program is Sarah Dawsey. The loyal volunteer cadre she has assembled is a function of both the interest of the service work and of Dawsey herself. On my first trip over to Cape Island in 2005 to build the turtle hatcheries, I met a contract employee, Billy Shaw, who traps predators of the loggerhead nests. On our second day of work, Billy, a long-term friend of Sarah, gave me his executive summary of her: "A wonderful human being." He described her capacity to work as incredible and, despite her small frame, challenged us to arm wrestle her. Billy had been a mentor for Sarah when she was a teenager in the Youth Conservation Corps (YCC) program. As a child, Sarah had gone out on the water with her father clamming, but it wasn't until the YCC—when she learned about birds and turtles from a YCC leader, Bobby Simpson—that wildlife became her passion. In her third year of YCC, she worked with Billy Shaw and Ruth Betcher. These positions were summer jobs, but she came back to the turtle program every year. Since her YCC days, Sarah has worked on Cape Island for twenty-four years. Billy told me about the days before they had ATVs on the island, when they used to walk the beach carrying a bucket and tools for nest relocation. Later, Sarah also told me about those early days:

> *It was interesting. We had a jeep at the time. Of course, as you can only imagine it did not fare well. It was held together by duct tape, primarily. I remember in my first year out there that the steering did not work for half the season, and being the YCC I was the one that had to turn the tires. So, we were going down the road, and I would have to get out and turn the tires by hand, and you can imagine the sandspurs. Interesting.*

While discussing the difficulty of the work on Cape Island, Sarah shared that some of the more recent years have been difficult because of the "break," the new inlet separating Cape Island into two parts. There have been previous breaks, including the one caused by Hurricane Hugo that is now closed.

Also in the 2005 season, I had the opportunity to spend a couple of days in the usual work of the turtle crews: identifying and recording crawls and false crawls on the beaches, locating nests, determining need for relocation, excavation of required nests and transfer to hatcheries or sites with reduced danger of erosion. Eggs were counted, recorded and recounted. Nests left in place (in situ) or moved to another location were caged to protect against predation (raccoons) but in such a way as to allow hatchlings to exit after emerging from the nest.

Cape Island

A large portion of the work for the turtle program is relocation of nests that have been placed by the female loggerheads in areas where they will be washed over by high tides or completely destroyed due to erosion. This conservation technique practiced by biologists on nesting beaches throughout the world is not without controversy. One argument against relocation of vulnerable nests is the tampering with natural selection—the idea that these doomed eggs, if relocated, will produce adult females that will continue to locate their nests in nonviable areas. An assumption of this argument is that some turtles are "bad nesters" while others are "good." A study in 2005 of loggerheads on an Australian nesting beach looked at whether this was the case. It was found that over 80 percent of nesting loggerheads selected at least one unsuccessful nest site during the season (nesters averaged a little under four nests per season). On the dynamic beaches that loggerheads nest, like Cape Island, there are tradeoffs for nest placement: low nests are vulnerable to seawater inundation and erosion, while nests farther inland face the threat of hatchling disorientation and higher rates of predation and desiccation of eggs, adult females and hatchlings. There are other arguments against nest relocation, and the scientific discussion will continue.

During that first season, I also had the opportunity to spend a night with staff and volunteers on the island, working and witnessing the events occurring during the night. That August night was one to remember, with the sea turtle trifecta observed: females crawling out of the surf, a female on her nest laying eggs and emerged hatchlings making the run to the surf. It was a memorable night, one to be rivaled two years later when I experienced another night on the island. On this August night, we patiently watched at a hatchery until several nests "boiled" and then escorted the hatchlings to the water. We encountered a different sort of excitement about 2:00 a.m. when Sarah Dawsey roused us all from our tents to head for a low spot in the dunes due to severe thunderstorms. We spent the rest of the night pelted by the rain with lightning striking all around, huddled as a group in a "prayer" circle.

Not scared away by the previous experience, I signed up for a third turtle night on August 1, 2008. Our crew was fortunate to not have the storm excitement of the previous year, though the evening started out with a solid shower for an hour and a half. We walked over to the hatcheries soon thereafter in the dark and noticed that the movement of hatchlings to the sea had begun without us. The ghost crabs had already taken their toll of several hatchlings, so we began the effort to provide a safe passage for the infant loggerheads to the water. As in the previous year, it became the expedient practice to collect the hatchlings in a bag and carry them to just above the water's edge. The pace quickened suddenly with a wave of hatchlings coming out of the hatchery. In taking stock later, we realized that six nests hatched out about the same time. The wave of hatchlings was so big that my bag became full and certainly had over a hundred little turtles. All in all that night, we probably observed a couple hundred turtles making the plunge into the ocean, though we also noted a few others killed or mortally wounded by the ghost crabs.

While trapping has reduced raccoon predation on Cape Island, the population of the Atlantic ghost crab (*Ocypode quadrata*) has correspondingly grown. The varied diet of raccoons includes ghost crabs, and the mammals' reduction has resulted in the large number of this crustacean once known as "the fleet-footed one of white." These are true crabs, belonging to the same family as fiddler crabs. Ghost crabs have adapted more successfully to living on land than any other South Carolina crab, only returning to the sea's edge to wet their gills or release eggs for their larval development. The crabs tunnel up to four feet deep into the sand and can easily reach the eggs of sea turtle nests. The greater numbers of ghost crabs present a lethal obstacle to the emerging hatchlings when they make their scramble to the water, and on this night in August 2008, the volunteers worked to protect the hatchlings from these predators, which would grab hatchlings and pull them down into their burrows for consumption. Volunteers have a visceral reaction to this crustacean's instinctual predation, in strong contrast to the nurturing of the hatchlings, helping to increase the chances of hatchling survival beyond transporting them to the water in bags. The linking of these three animals—raccoons, loggerhead turtles and ghost crabs—illustrates the complex food web of the natural world.

When the hatching was done, we traveled south on the ATVs to search for turtle crawls. After arriving late for several nests, with the business done and the turtles long gone, we finally found a turtle already started on digging her nest cavity. Silently we approached and observed this marvelous and instinctual ritual. The dexterity of the rear flippers was surprising and extraordinary. The process went on for some time, and then the turtle began the dropping of her eggs into the carefully prepared chamber. She entered her trance-like state, enabling us to move closer to observe. The nest would require relocating the next day, and I had the privilege to dig up and count her 118 eggs, excavate a new chamber for the eggs and rebury them. We did our part to help these future turtles beat the odds in surviving on this strand.

Jerry Tupacz pointed out on the nesting female a significant scar: a large chunk from her right front shell was missing. He speculated that this was the result of a shark attack. As she walked out to the beach toward the water, Jerry used a scanner to electronically probe for tags. In fact, he found three, and the scanner was able to access a tag's number. With inquiry through the sea turtle network, it was found that this turtle had had a false crawl earlier in the season on Wassaw Island, part of Georgia's Wassaw National Wildlife Refuge; but what else of her life? Did this turtle dig out of her mother's nest chamber on Cape Island or some other nearby beach? What currents has she plied in her travels around the Atlantic gyre? How did she survive the violent trauma, and by what attacker? Has she nested on Cape Island previously? Would she remember this encounter with humans on Cape Island? I have no doubt that we all will.

Loggerhead hatchling on Cape Island heading toward the ocean.

JUNE 10, 2006

Low tide 1:45 p.m. Predicted winds SW 10 knots in the morning, shifting to S 10–15 knots in the afternoon.

The vessel *Hatteras* is tied up to the government dock used by USFWS. The crew has been making engine repairs and plans to leave within the hour. This workhorse with a large deck and heavy lift transports vehicles, heavy equipment and even tanks. At 8:50 a.m. we are sailing out Jeremy Creek, across the ICW and then Clubhouse Creek. It is a quiet downwind sail through the creek and past Jeremy Island. The reverse current of Island Cut does not impede our progress on the reaches and runs today, yet gives me pause to ponder a tragic event in this narrow waterway.

On May 24, 1911, Captain William Leland, in his vessel *Rufus Gibbs*, was returning from Georgetown after delivering a load of shells. He was towing another boat, the *John S. Gibbs*. As he and his black crew were passing through Island Cut, one of the crewmen, David Simpson, fell overboard. It was later speculated that Simpson had been asleep along the gunwale when he went into the water. The tide was rapidly falling, and when Simpson came to the surface, he was far astern. Leland was a strong swimmer and dove in to rescue his crewman. He had actually gone past the submerged Simpson when the drowning man rose for the second time. Leland finally reached his crewman when his head bobbed above the surface for the third and last time. Simpson grabbed Leland around the neck, and they both disappeared beneath the surface. Efforts by the remaining crew to launch a bateau and attempt a rescue were in vain.

The tragedy of the loss of the young Leland, only twenty-six years of age, compounded the family's grief over the death of his mother, Ann Boleyn Baker Leland, the previous year. Leland was awarded posthumously the Carnegie Medal in 1912. David Simpson's loss was memorialized in the placing of his name on the Lowcountry Seamen's Memorial at the Ashley Landing in McClellanville. Ironically, an oversight resulted in leaving off William Leland's name.

At the junction with Skrine Creek, a moored vessel observed this spring is now sunk, with just the upper part of the cabin exposed. Soon we're out into Muddy Bay, and at two hours after high tide it is a large body of water. Our course is an arc around an oyster reef on the north bank and then toward the abandoned observation tower on a small marsh island. The lighthouses are prominent to the southeast. We're on a broad reach, heading out Horsehead Creek; it is quiet, calm and steady sailing in the light but consistent breeze as we make Cape Romain Harbor, the large sound behind Cape Island. There is a boat here and there as we set course for Cowpen Point in a shifting wind. We sail past the dock on the point where the aluminum USFWS boat is secured and land on the other side of the point.

It is near this location where an uncomfortable but humorous story occurred that Sarah Dawsey recounted for me. The episode happened during one of the working nights on the island when the turtle program was using non-self-releasing hatcheries, requiring workers to stay out every night until all the nests were hatched out. They ran into a couple of young men who were stranded on the island when their boat floated off with the tide. They had called someone to come and were waiting to be picked up. Sarah recalled that one of them was running down the sandspur-covered track barefoot, wearing only a bathing suit, and flailing away at the hordes of biting insects. Waiting for their rescue, the two men stayed in the water for protection, with just their heads above the surface. They surely learned about the importance of adequately securing their boat, as have I and many other Lowcountry boaters by similar unsettling experiences.

Near *Kingfisher* sits a small outboard high on the beach, left here for reasons unknown. It is time to explore the Cowpen area on foot and with my camera. There are piles of debris by the dock, and I recognize the remains of the USFWS shed that used to house tools and gear for the loggerhead conservation program. The shed is a casualty of the application of the Wilderness Act in the refuge. Since the majority of the refuge was designated as Class I Wilderness Area in the early 1970s, the USFWS has taken a proactive stance in complying with these guidelines, and several changes have been made. Only one ATV trip is allowed to the beach and back each day. The shed for equipment storage has also been taken down. The loggerhead management program has, in general, strived to have as limited impact as possible on the island. While the Wilderness Act does not allow for certain equipment within its borders, the guidelines are balanced within an endangered species program, accepting the reality that some equipment is required for management. Sarah Dawsey referenced the minimal tool policy when discussing the changes.

The road here is kept "mowed" by the passage of ATVs from the dock to the turtle work on the beach, but it is still quite vegetated. Along the road, large numbers of sea ox-eyes are flowering, and yuccas display their yellow blooms. A snake slithers off the road, and I am reminded of my garb—shorts and sandals. This is my first time walking this narrow track. I am used to traveling along here with a higher perspective, standing on the ATV-towed trailers with the loggerhead turtle program. I find a narrow crossing between this road and the water to make the return walk to *Kingfisher* via the beach along the backside of the island.

I launch *Kingfisher* and begin the sail to the North Point, staying close to the sound side of Cape Island. A creek runs into the marsh not too far from the beach along Cowpen Point and is an access to the remaining freshwater impoundment now reverted to salt marsh. The run to the North Point is longer than anticipated. Close to the end of the island, it is clear how much the inlet has narrowed between Cape and Murphy Islands. On the landing, I miscalculate the depth of the drop-off and get wet up to my waist while stepping ashore.

In the past, this channel was the outlet of choice for commercial fishermen heading offshore. From this inlet on July 24, 1968, the forty-five-foot trawler *Eugenie* was heading outward bound toward the blackfish banks off Georgetown and into an awaiting mystery. Once at the fishing grounds, and having set their fishing traps and anchored for the night in calm seas, the two-man crew—owner John A. Solomons Jr. and his black striker, Leroy Simpson—were in communication and sight of another trawler when they turned in. The next morning, in continued calm weather, there was no sign of the *Eugenie*, though her traps were still on the bottom. An extensive sea and air search came up empty, including an electronic search by a naval minesweeper. No wreckage from the *Eugenie* was ever found. Extensive speculation persisted, but forty years later there is still no answer to this sea mystery. Both Solomons and Simpson are memorialized on the Lowcountry Seamen's Memorial.

A boat is fishing in the inside inlet, but *Kingfisher* is the lone hull on the inlet's beach as I make the walk around the point and head to the turtle hatcheries. In April, I worked on building these hatcheries for my second season. The volunteer crew on the first day of work anticipated seeing the remains of a rare find along the coast: the skeleton of a humpback whale. Marine biologists determined that this whale was killed by a collision with a ship. Much effort had been made to recover the skeleton, but its sheer size and weight made recovery very difficult; the whale was estimated to be forty-five feet long and weighed thirty tons. When we arrived on the scene, we first saw a section of vertebrae about the size of my waist lying on the beach. Around the low-water line, the pelvis of the whale was partially buried in the sand. Most significant was the jawbone relocated high on the beach—about fifteen feet long, curved and weighing about five hundred pounds.

Today, there is no sign of the whale jawbone or vertebrae—I hope they have been safely recovered for conservation and display—but the pelvis is still in the shifting sands between low and high water. Many loggerhead nests along the dunes have been protected in place, and many others have been located to Hatchery #1. I take a swim, eat lunch and relax on a log, appreciating the solitude and remoteness of this exquisite barrier island. Into my meditation seeps the recognition that the wind is picking up. I am hoping it is veering to the south, or else I will have lots of windward work on the way back to the entrance to Horsehead Creek.

Arriving back at the point, I note an ancient potshard lying, along with the shells, at the waterline. The fisherman continues his pursuit in the inlet along Murphy Island, and he moves and resets his anchor while I rig *Kingfisher*. The wind has really picked up beyond the prediction of the marine forecast, and my hope for a reach back up the harbor is dashed. It appears that it will be a long beat to windward back to Horsehead Creek. Adjustments to flatten out the sail in the strong wind are required before getting underway a little before 2:00 p.m. Beginning the thrash to windward, I sheet in and evaluate: there will be no sitting on the side but full hiking out for an abdominal workout. *Kingfisher* is sailing well but not flat at all, and I conserve energy with the sail trim for this long haul.

I decide to stay on the Cape Island side, since the chart indicates more water. We're getting help from the start of the incoming tide, but conversely, the opposition of the strong wind with the tide is creating a steep chop to knock through. Occasionally waves are coming over *Kingfisher*'s bow and my body. We continue to beat up the Cape Island shore, searching for smoother water but without success. I am rewarded by a close encounter with a sizable loggerhead that takes a peek and dives. I also notice that one of the clips holding the sail on the boom has popped off; this is no big thing until a second adjoining clip also comes off. Now there is a noticeable strain on the nearest clips and, clearly, on the sail. It is worth worrying about and considering a repair. Grabbing a piece of line off my hiking stick, I steer head to wind for the quick jury rig, but the wind and waves quickly turn the bow away from the wind, thwarting my attempt. There is a similar result on my second attempt. I am startled during this effort by a boat rounding my stern twenty yards to leeward and see that it is USFWS enforcement personnel coming to check me out. I am wearing my PFD and wave to them. They appear satisfied as they head off.

Landing would make the repair a cinch, but as we head into Cowpen we run into a shoal. Not wanting to bear off and lose ground to make this shore, I steer out again for my course to Horsehead Creek, hoping I can make it to those calmer waters. The incoming tide and longer port tacks help me to complete my almost hour-long sail across the harbor and into the creek. Once in the protected waters, I lash down the unclipped sail and sheet in onto a close reach. It is great sailing, and *Kingfisher* breaks surface tension onto a long plane in the steady wind. It is not long before we're skimming across the waters of Muddy Bay and arcing around the north shore oyster reef. Looking back into Skrine Creek, more of the sunken vessel is exposed.

Soon we're entering Clubhouse Creek, and an hour and a half after low tide the creek is quite narrow. The tide is still favorable before the reversal ahead in Island Cut, and bends in the creek to the southwest will require more windward work. It is a run through here, but the remnant of Jeremy Island to the south is blocking my wind. We reach the turn to the south, with the course upwind and against the tide. The forces opposing me are joined by the Jeremy Island greenhead flies, sensing my two-handed occupation with sailing as an opportunity for attacks. There is good progress in the first section, but I pay the price for being greedy by holding a tack too far in the attempt to squeeze by the western creek bank. I encounter some difficulty in freeing *Kingfisher* of the shore's clutches. There is a little relief in the next creek section, but soon we are battling against wind and tide. We are suddenly aground on the east creek bank and wait to get off until another boat passes in the narrow waters. Continuing the upwind climb, the entrance to the waterway leading to the ICW appears.

We are now on a beam reach with the luxury of the rising tide and cruising rapidly. We pass the little island at the creek mouth entering into the ICW and head toward home. Turning into Jeremy Creek, we still enjoy the following tide and wind. Fifty yards from the landing, I round up, head to wind, for the sail drop and coast to a dead-stick landing at the dock. All appears normal for unrigging and pulling out *Kingfisher*. Yet on a stopover at the Village Museum a previous nagging strain to my upper back inflames to a burning pain. Cape Island and its waters have taken their toll on this aging sailor. The specific actions of digging holes for posts at the hatcheries in April and sheeting in the sail on my long upwind battle in the Cape Romain Harbor this afternoon are the sources for this overuse injury. It appears that the maintenance and repair of *Kingfisher* will need to be complemented with rest and therapy for this new ailment, one that will keep us off these waters for a little while.

September 3, 2006

Low tide 9:30 a.m. Predicted winds E 5 knots in the morning, then E 10–15 knots in the afternoon.

I am off in Jeremy Creek at 8:00 a.m. on an outgoing tide, in a very light west-northwest wind. The wind dies upon reaching the ICW, so we just drift with the outgoing tide into Town Creek. Two kayaks are coming from behind, and even though the paddlers have set a leisurely pace, they reel us in fairly quickly. A Beaufort man is paddling a strip plank boat. The kayakers laugh when I show them my towline. They easily pass the windless *Kingfisher* and offer encouragement with the wind to come. Their easy pass makes me a bit antsy, so I rig my bamboo tiller extension. I begin some paddling, which I alternate with using the paddle to hold out my boom, when a hint of some wind almost has me sailing. But we are moving slowly as the kayaks disappear ahead. For the moment, I realize that I am thinking about what lies ahead rather than right now. A dark cloud is forming to the north, and I recall the predawn shower and lightning.

The wind's turn to the south is encouraging, and past the junction of creeks, the dark figure of a wood stork flies parallel to my course to the east. Then a second wood stork crosses my stern, displaying its distinct black-and-white wings. As we pass the mouth of Key Creek, two outboards roar into the waterway and a pod of dolphins passes. Ahead, the two kayaks are on the shore of Raccoon Key. The wind is finally around to the east, and we are slowly reaching the point and the inlet leading to the bay and ocean. The slow sail is now hampered by the already turned tide.

We are finally out at the relatively late time of 10:00 a.m. It is clear at the outlet that we will be going against the current, and beating to the east we lose some ground each tack. The bay is smooth, making for gentle sailing. I keep *Kingfisher* out of the dredged channel and close to the beach, but the incoming flow is evident even close to the shore. Where the channel turns to the southeast, I try the port tack, hoping to lee bow the incoming tide. We tack and head back toward Raccoon Key. We maintain this course in the vicinity of the beach, tacking off and on. A black cloud still hovers in the north, and in the event of a thunderstorm, I can quickly beach *Kingfisher* and reduce my profile. But all is fine now, and as we continue to beat to windward, I count five shrimp trawlers working offshore. There are no other craft in view.

The breeze is slowly increasing, and *Kingfisher* is picking up speed. I'm sitting on the side and sheeting in closer, taking advantage more and more of the clam cleats installed on either side of the deck for fastening the sheet. People are on the beach around the center of the island, having accessed the island by a tidal creek. We continue tacking on and off, and the weather provokes continued concern. The profile and white sand of the beach of Lighthouse Island, the proposed destination, is in sight. The plan is to land and walk to the east end of this barrier and back. The shoals of Key Inlet lie ahead, so we stay off, looking for the passage observed on our first trip here. The channel between the shoals bearing northeast becomes clear, and we tack through this section, making it inside without problem.

The challenging part of the sail for the day is over: beaching on Lighthouse Island and sailing downwind later will be routine. Yet I am pondering something else: continuing with the upwind sail to the south tip of Cape Island. The breeze is steady, and the windward progress has continued to improve. At the west end of Lighthouse Island inside the shoals, I recall a channel close to the island's tip and head *Kingfisher* up to closehauled to work through here. Again, I find incoming tide with a moderate current opposing my course. We are tacking off and on between the shore and the shoals in this battle. The starboard tack toward shore presents the sight of dark clouds continuing to threaten in the north. The port tack away from land reveals a bipolar image of sun, reflecting off the ocean, clear sky and the shiny sands of the beach ahead. The departure from the planned sail means the contemplation of a complete circumnavigation of Cape Island. The rounding of the cape has been in my plans for some time, and I've considered what would be the right conditions. The marine elements today are not ideal. Heading toward shore on starboard tack, the dark seems more pronounced, and the collective of pelicans and terns also present a dark cast. I look for a sign, from birds or elsewhere: to go on or to bear off and return to plan A? Dark clouds of rain are more imminent, yet the breeze is firm, and there is still no sign of lightning. So we carry on to windward.

Every port tack heading offshore puts me on an intersecting course with a trawler pulling her nets. We never get that close, but our proximity and pace create an unusual bond between sailing craft and diesel trawler. Several times we approach again, and the eye contact of helmsmen seems more than imaginary. The fixed constants of this seascape are the lighthouse towers—white and black, and red. As we make progress, their juxtaposition changes the geometric triangulation. Cape Point is now in view, and it is time to survey and enter this inlet, which is not on my chart and remained unnamed in my conversations with locals. This inlet was formed in 1996 when Hurricane Bertha passed closely, amputating the southwestern part of Cape Island. In fact, the new inlet is a resurfacing of the major inlet along here in the past: the Cape Romain inlet, where vessels would enter Cape Romain Harbor. Gene Morrison, from his teenage years, remembers the opening as Lighthouse Inlet, and its channel was deep enough for the passage of shrimp boats to head out and shrimp off the cape shoals.

I look offshore to the south, realizing the exposure and potential for tragedy in these waters, and wonder about the sandbar where Rob Mallard and Dave Nelson experienced a day and night of life and death that they will never forget. Having gone for a fishing trip in November 2005 to a familiar sandbar over a mile off the coast here, a hot spot for large redfish, they experienced the dread of boaters—a loosened anchor and an adrift boat. Mallard was closest and thought he could easily swim to the drifting craft. He soon realized that not only could he not reach the boat, but also he could not swim against the current and waves to regain the sandbar. His only alternative was to swim to Lighthouse Island; fortunately, a daily routine of swimming contributed to his reaching the barrier island over two hours later.

His friend Nelson was stranded on the sandbar and was convinced he had just seen his friend drown. The tide was rising, and he prepared his six-foot sand spike with his rod and T-shirt tied to the top for the rising tide and wind. By 2:00 p.m. he was chest deep in the waters over the sandbar. The earlier unseasonably warm weather had turned with the shift to strong and much colder northeast winds.

So the friends, cold, exposed and fearful for each other's lives, were stranded. Their lateness triggered both worry in their wives and a call to a good friend, fishing boat captain Champ Smith. Champ and his fellow fishing guide, Bootsey Wilson, went out on Wilson's boat to aid the Coast Guard search already initiated. It was after dark, the wind and waves had increased and the temperatures had dropped to the mid-forties. Smith and Wilson were familiar with the sandbar, but finding it in the dark was another story. They were given instructions to not interfere with the official search, but when this search was called off later due to dangerous conditions, they headed back out. Navigating out through Muddy Bay and beyond with a searchlight, they were preparing to head out to the sandbar when their light on Lighthouse Island revealed a cold and excited Mallard. Once onboard, he implored them to get out to the bar for his friend. After a search of about twenty-five minutes, they spotted the white T-shirt and picked up Nelson at about 1:00 a.m., suffering from exhaustion and hypothermia. The exhausted and chilled friends cried all the way on the long ride to McClellanville.

We finally pass and leave the trawler in our lee—she would not be entering this way. Earlier this year, during a turtle program trip, I visually surveyed the inlet from Cape Point. Today, there are a couple of boats inside in view, indicating water deep enough for *Kingfisher*. There are significant shoals on the east or Cape Point side, so our course is to stay on the Lighthouse Island side for the inlet passage. Not wanting to give too much windward advantage away, we stay on the edge of the waves of the east shoals, and these breakers are small and no problem for *Kingfisher*. A blue outboard is moving to set an anchor on the Lighthouse Island side. It is bouncing around as we glide by to windward with the incoming tide. And then we are in, sailing on smooth, protected waters inside of Cape Point. There is one other craft inside: a blue and white boat, with a cabin suggesting overnight qualities and a small johnboat tethered to the stern. I learn later that this is the handcrafted vessel of Tommy Graham, champion of the lighthouses. I head for the inside

Cape Island

beach of Cape Point, and the landing appears a cinch, with a steep drop-off and sand bank. After landing, I leave the sail up and grab my lunch. It's after 1:00 p.m., and I'm famished.

The solitude is soon ended by an outboard coming out to the point from behind Lighthouse Island. A couple with a young child lands nearby. Soon, another boat arrives, followed by a pair of outboards. This is clearly a choice landing spot. It is Sunday of Labor Day weekend, so the company is expected. This group has come here in the tradition of summer Cape Island parties.

Cape parties have been a part of the McClellanville social scene for years. In past times, a large group would make the seven-mile trip from the village on larger vessels. One example shows the scale of these outings. On August 26, 1929, about 110 people embarked on two vessels, *Happy Days* and *Carolina*, for the voyage out through the creeks to the island. A number of the guests were from out of town. This party was hosted by Mr. and Mrs. Ludie A. Beckman. On this day, while party participants frolicked in the surf, men pulled seine nets and collected oysters to provide fresh seafood to be cooked

Shell assemblage on Cape Point.

on the beach. The picnic feast was served under a large canvas canopy. The return trip was accompanied by the singing of songs.

The current Cape Island party is a flurry of activity as the groups land boats, work on anchoring and move gear to the beach. The men with surf gear head across the point to fish the Cape Point surf, the women and youngest children set up sunning and picnic areas by their boats and the older children head up the backside to explore. I, too, walk along the backside and cut across the point, skirting the edge of a large salt flat. It appears that the point could easily split off from the rest of Cape Island and become another isolated islet.

Once over to the beach and ocean, there arises on the high-tide line an incredible array of flotsam and jetsam—shells, driftwood, weathered cans and plastic bottles. It is an impressive visual display. There are also fresh ATV tracks from the turtle conservation crew earlier today. Walking around the point, I stop to say hello and chat with one of the fishermen. They are going after spot tail bass and mention a fine fish caught here recently. They came through a shower on their way out but saw no lightning. He comments on how it must be a fine day for sailing, and I agree. I look offshore for a glimpse of the breakers on the Cape Romain Shoals and survey the nearer shoals and inlet as I complete my walk around the point and back to *Kingfisher*.

It is now time for contemplation of the return voyage, with several options: a) sail inside through one of several inside passages, downwind and easy with an incoming tide; b) head out the inlet and retrace my morning journey downwind along Lighthouse Island and Raccoon Key; or c) head out the inlet and round Cape Point, sailing north up the island for a completion of the outside passage by coming in the North Point inlet. I imagined my rounding day of the cape would have a south or southwest breeze, but already today I've made a large commitment getting here with the beat all the way up from Five Fathom Creek. I still hesitate, since there will be some further windward work and negotiating of the shoals. Though the swell is small, we will have to make it round to the point where *Kingfisher* can close reach parallel to shore on the course north.

I secure my gear and raise sail. Casting off, we head toward the inlet on the port tack in the protected waters. The figure-eight knot has slipped from the end of my sheet and pulls through the ratchet block. I carefully negotiate heading up without unreeving the sheet from any more of the blocks on the boom and re-rig without hitting any of the Cape Island party boats. I also pull on my lifejacket and begin the sail out the inlet. The course is to get to windward, but the east shoals and breakers are an obstruction to doing so. I pick a promising place and begin to work through, watching the waves ahead as I commit to going out and around. We're doing fine, though in one trough the daggerboard touches and must be pulled up while simultaneously bearing off a little. Passing over a couple of swells, we are clear and crank up automatically to closehauled with the board going down. There is no question about going for the rounding now; the conditions are fine, with small seas and steady east wind. We hold the port tack, noting the breakers ahead on another set of shoals, and come about before the waves onto the starboard tack. It's clear that we will need a couple more tacks to weather the eastward curvature of the island. We hold toward the beach breakers and tack early to keep off this lee shore.

Kingfisher is performing wonderfully in the small sea, easily riding over these smooth peaks. The ocean is opening up ahead, and a final tack takes us to the lay line. We work to make the curve of the island to the north and soon see clear, with a large gathering of pelicans and seabirds as witness. The surf fishermen are far astern. The point of sail is a glorious close reach, parallel to the beach and about one hundred yards off. The wind is ten to twelve knots, and it is sunny, with no dark clouds around. The ocean color is more beautiful and striking than I've seen on the South Carolina coast in some time. The waves are splashing me a little, but the air and water temperatures with the sun and wind are perfect stimuli. Water is beginning to accumulate in the cockpit, and I pull the cork for the cockpit bailer, placing the stopper in a zippered pocket for safekeeping and later use, since I will not be on this point of sail and speed the rest of the afternoon. But at this moment, all is wonderful on this fine cruise along the shoreline. No marine life appears with me, except for a stray cannonball jellyfish.

We are past the lower southern end of the island with limited areas of dunes, and then we pass the upland and established pine forest. We round another bend in the beach, noticeable from this perspective and on the ATV rides, and continue to reach to the north. Occasionally the sheet goes in the cleat, but it feels more comfortable in my hand in steering through waves. A trawler is ahead near the inlet, and our progress has us abeam of the loggerhead hatcheries. The trawler is actually going in around the North Point about a half mile ahead. There are clear views of Murphy and Cedar Islands to the north, and I look forward to sailing to these destinations soon. Birds are gathered at the point. There is a confused and small surf stirred up by the tide rolling in this inlet. We're still on a close reach and almost in from the ocean. Looking over to leeward under the sail, both to see if I'm past the small point and to notice what birds are watching my entrance to the inlet, we bear off and are immediately hit by the onrushing tide-line waves that come over the bow. *Kingfisher* receives a couple inches of water in the cockpit as the welcome into the inlet. It has been about fifty-five minutes from point to point.

In rounding this point, the canoe-like *Kingfisher* lies between the courses of two famous and extraordinary voyages: the voyage of the paper canoe by Nathaniel Holmes Bishop and the voyage of the *Liberdade* by Joshua Slocum and his family. Bishop started in Quebec in 1874 in an eighteen-foot wooden canoe accompanied by a New Jersey waterman attempting to travel south by inland waterways until reaching the Gulf of Mexico. Abandoning this canoe and crew for a canoe built of laminated paper near Troy, New York, on the Hudson River, he continued south, rowing his craft through waterways small and large. Thirteen years later, and approaching from the south, came Joshua Slocum. A merchant ship captain sailing with his young family, Slocum was master of the full-rigged ship *Aquidneck* that had gone aground on shoals off the Brazilian coast—a total loss. Rather than board another vessel for the trip home as passengers, Slocum and his family salvaged what wood and hardware they could from the wreck and set out to build a vessel for a sailing voyage home. While stretching the term "canoe," the thirty-five-foot *Liberdade* was built to handle the ocean passage. After a voyage lasting fifty-three days, the *Liberdade* made landfall at Cape Romain. These two historical courses come within a mile of meeting at this point where *Kingfisher* presently sails.

Into the inside waters we're immediately off and running. The trawler is anchored behind Cape Island. The tide is flowing in strongly, and we stay on the Murphy Island side. My hard work has me sailing now with riches gained: wind and tide at my back and depth of water everywhere. This is the most water I've seen in this sound—Cape Romain Harbor—and this body of water's large scale becomes apparent. All along there are large rafts of gulls taking the place of shoals. I note the location of the Alligator Creek entrance but sail on to the entrance to the Casino Creek system. There is a fisherman to the south at what the chart shows to be a twenty-foot hole as we enter the creek mouth, continuing to sail downwind with the tide. I note the mouth of Mill Creek on the north side, and two boats roar out of the creek into the harbor toward the south.

At the junction between the Congaree Boat and Casino Creeks, we take Congaree to the southwest. It is a wide creek, and I recall sailing through the previous week. We pass the creek heading to the south, past the observation tower and into Muddy Bay. I am on the same return passage similar to that last sail, and with the incoming tide still flooding and an onshore breeze, I am thinking again about the Joe and Ben Creek that I missed a week ago. The small entrance is ahead, and though tiny, the chart shows it going all the way through to the northern part of Muddy Bay. We head directly in, running along in the very narrow waterway. It continues to become narrower, and soon my boom and sail are brushing the cordgrass. It is getting tighter, and navigating the creek's bends is quite difficult. A fork appears at a crab pot float, quite out of place. I guess the port fork and see right away that it is wrong; unable to turn quickly in the tight quarters, we end up in the grass. Back paddling is tough against the wind, but we are finally out. We're committed, having come down tide and downwind some distance already. Sailing back out as we entered is not an option, and paddling out would be difficult. So we continue going downwind and down tide in what little channel is apparent.

We are getting deeper into this marsh morass; the creek is petering out, and dead cordgrass is becoming an obstruction slowing us down. We are slowed and stuck at one point and, with much effort, are extricated with paddling. But then we are stuck again, and all paddling efforts are in vain. So it is out of the boat and into the water to turn the hull manually. We are free but can't turn. At this point, I am wet and muddy, the deck is covered with cordgrass and we are firmly bemired in this vast marshland with shallow tepid waters. I stand on deck and survey the scene, trying to detect the presence of a creek—if it can be called that any longer—in the sea of marsh ahead. The open water of Muddy Bay appears in the distance. Sailing through no longer seems an option. It is time to drop the sail, pull the board out and bring up the rudder. I begin to pull *Kingfisher* along by the bowline while wading in the abdomen-deep water, losing and then retrieving a sandal. The bottom is thankfully oyster free, but this method seems too slow and laborious. I stop to retrieve a reliable old blue length of webbing that I've used since 1977, but I never seem to notice when my reading glasses are swallowed up.

Changing the propulsion plan, I sit on the bow and begin paddling, still slow but more efficient. I use my legs and feet outstretched to divert the floating dead *Spartina* like a bizarre Lowcountry icebreaker. We are making progress toward Muddy Bay and hoping for an outlet. We make it past a section of grass and then find a little more open area. Water is flowing toward me, a sign of water coming in from Muddy Bay. I ponder raising sail here but decide to paddle out to open water. An outboard goes by as we make it across a little bar at the edge of the creek and paddle out far enough to get the bow into the wind and raise sail. It's up, and I bear off to head home. Taking stock psychologically, I am humbled again—completing this circumnavigation required a bit more effort due to the final ordeal of the Joe and Ben Creek passage. Joe and Ben must be laughing hysterically somewhere. My intention to use this shortcut on the chart resulted in quite an ordeal and ultimately was a lesson learned.

Later in the month, Gene Morrison shared with me that the Joe and Ben Creek has gradually closed in the last forty years. He related a recent experience about another familiar creek:

> I had crab traps in this one year, and right up to the end of it there is a hole six feet deep that I had crab traps in, and it was three and four feet all the way in there. Anyway, I quit crabbing—I did that for a couple of years, and decided that it was not anything I wanted to do. I just went up there to go behind the beach to walk across the beach and fish the front beach. And I was running along wide open with the boat and was going across where I thought was six feet of water, and ran hard aground. I ran right up on the bank, hard and dry, where it was six feet the year before. The beach, the sand, had washed across the beach and filled it in. You get surprises like that sometimes.

Bob Baldwin, another commercial fisherman still making his living in the creek, had a different story about changing water depth:

> I got a good lesson in that this spring. Because there is a point down by Cape Romain that I grow clams on...I had bags there, and put a screen

Cape Island

out, and the screen did real well, so I only have a few bags left, mostly just screens there now. But anyway, I went there this spring, and it never was real wide, but you know fairly wide, so I jumped overboard to put the anchor out, and there wasn't any bottom there. The channel had moved in a little closer.

We are now in Island Cut with easy sailing and pick up the usual Jeremy Island flies. Before the turn to the west, we carry the course almost all the way to the grass before jibing. A boat manned by adolescent males passes back and forth. We make the turn at the Five Fathom Creek junction and then, with ease, reach the ICW. The landing is very busy on this holiday weekend, with other boats converging to haul out. I drop sail and, due to the traffic and crowd at the dock, land *Kingfisher* on the remains of the rock and mud beach to await our turn.

MARSH ISLAND

Hidden in the middle of Bulls Bay is a little, low-lying patch of sand and mud. Historically, it would not qualify as an island but instead as an underwater shoal for mariners to avoid. An 1859 U.S. Coast Survey preliminary chart of Bulls Bay shows this area as an underwater shoal called "Petrel Bank." Another chart shows this as "Vessel Reef Shoal," a name still used by some locals, indicating that a shipwreck may have occurred here. Once the shoal accreted enough to classify it as an island, several maps labeled it White Island. The name "marsh island" is used generically for all of the small and large rises of *Spartina alterniflora* marsh throughout the refuge and beyond. This Marsh Island is distinguished from many other small isles by its selection by the bird world as the location for colonial nesting. The selection seems a wise choice since the island is isolated from access by natural predators, particularly raccoons, and from the intrusion of man. It has special protection in CRNWR and is closed year-round by the South Carolina Department of Natural Resources.

The island has some beach areas around the east, south and western sides, but a good portion of the island is salt marsh that penetrates into the interior. The high ground is covered with mainly low vegetation. The nesting colonies cover sizable portions of the island. The largest populations are of brown pelicans, royal terns and assorted wading birds, including herons and egrets.

I sailed to the island for the first time in 2003 and was amazed at the concentration of bird life. I received an invitation from Felicia Sanders, state

DNR wildlife biologist for coastal projects, to participate in the annual survey

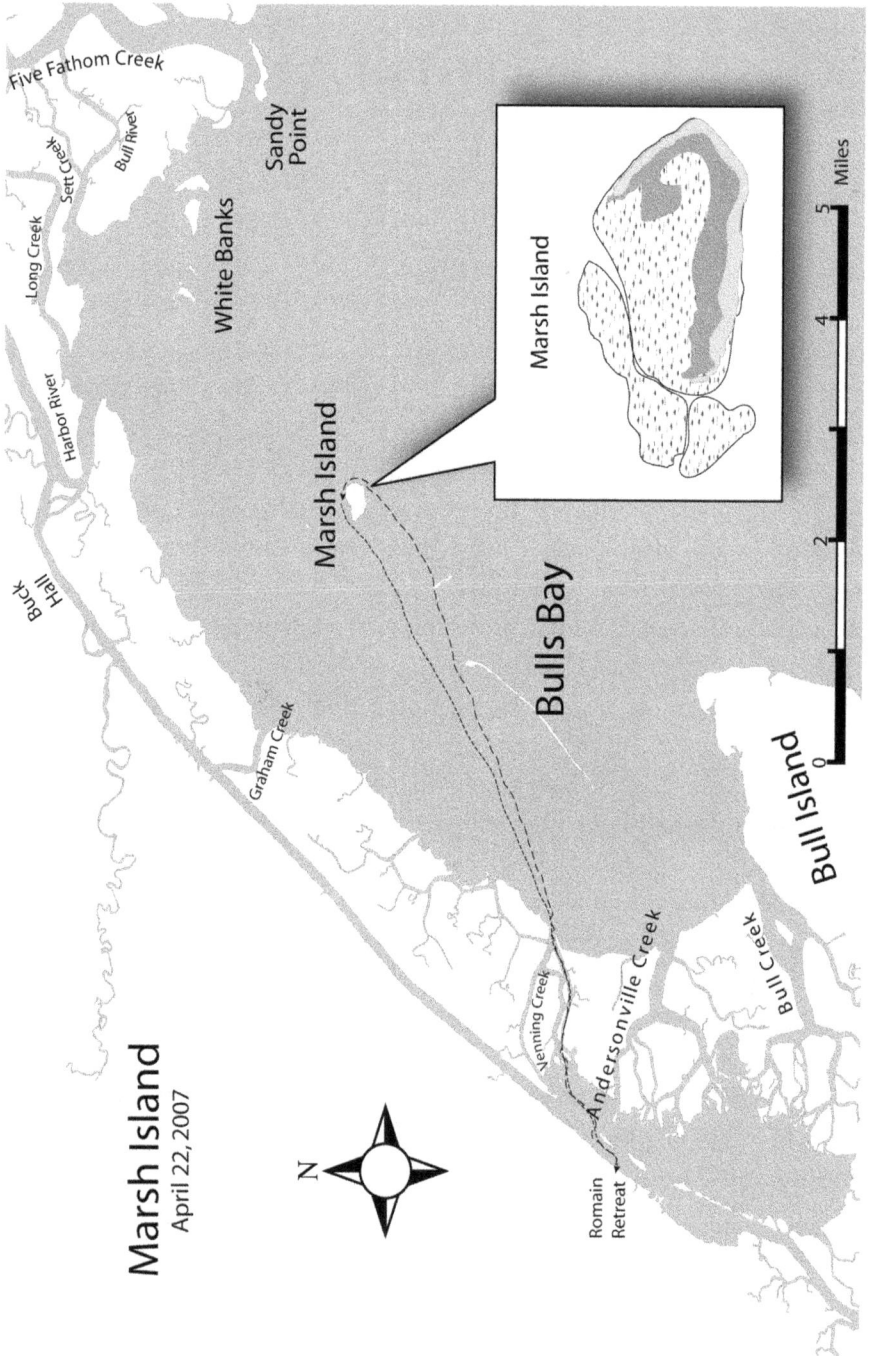

Marsh Island

of the nesting colony in 2006. Since this is a closed island, the opportunity to walk around and observe firsthand the colony and participate in the survey was a wish come true. We left out of Jeremy Creek on May 18, 2006, in two DNR boats, with the crew consisting of DNR staff Felicia Sanders and Mark Spinks, Kelly (DNR intern from Horry County Tech), Sarah Dawsey from CRNWR and volunteers Mary Katherine Martin, Neal Peterson and myself. This was my first meeting with Neal Peterson, the South African sailor who distinguished himself in the Around Alone singlehanded sailing event several years before and added his name to the roster of solo circumnavigators in the world. As fellow sailors, we hit it off right away.

Mark, in his DNR Boston Whaler, took the lead heading out Five Fathom Creek and across the bay, taking an indirect route due to the low tide. The wind was from the southwest and picking up to the forecasted fifteen to twenty knots; the ride was bumpy going across the bay. We finally made the turn to the northwest and headed toward the green of Marsh Island. Mark was searching for the channel running along the northeast side of the island. Without hitting bottom, we found the channel and made our landing. The boats were anchored on the edge of this sandy beach, and the incoming tide would ensure getting off easily.

Besides the survey, we would also put up more "Closed Area" signs. Felicia oriented us to the methodology of the survey—using counters, walking in "the line," counting to the right, etc. Brown pelicans would be the first colony for survey. We learned how to approach nests and where to step, particularly avoiding other nests (like those of laughing gulls). All our senses were alert as we initiated the survey. The pelican eggs were large, off-white and etched with light patterning. The hatched chicks were purple, leathery and noisy with their squawking, and I found myself transported to what a dinosaur nesting colony might have been like. I was missing one sense—smell—and being aroma-challenged was a benefit in these circumstances, since the nests also contained freshly regurgitated menhaden with an odor not for the weak of stomach. Some of the eggs had signs of piping. The survey crew moved in a line, methodically clicking, focused on the count, while brown pelicans took off from the nests and returned after we moved on. Upon finishing this section, we walked on to a larger section near the southeast side of the island.

The center of the island has an inner marsh, and isolated in the middle was a little bump of high ground where pelicans also nest. This high spot had been surveyed earlier. We walked parallel to the beach for this largest section of the pelican rookery. Kelly, the intern, on her first day of fieldwork, walked to my right. I heard a loud clopping noise nearby; a pelican stayed put on the nest and used this aggressive beak sound as a threatening display. It worked, since Kelly stopped, and she asked Felicia what to do. "Walk around" was the guidance, and we moved on from there. Finishing this section, we walked to the western side.

This was the area I viewed in my sail here in July 2003. The beach was covered in shells, and shoals stretched out from the shore. The royal tern colony resided here, but we bypassed this survey now and would pick it up on our return. One more small section of pelican colony remained for our survey; nearby, we saw another area of wading birds nesting: tricolor herons, common egrets, snowy egrets, cattle egrets and glossy ibis. After finishing the pelican section and moving over to prepare for the wading bird count, we saw an oystercatcher nest on the beach, the lightly colored and patterned eggs situated among shells. Felicia oriented us to distinguishing between the various eggs. The wading bird nests were located in some different vegetation that I was not used to seeing on other islands in the refuge: pokeweed. It has a bush-like structure, and obviously these birds were partial to its utility for nesting. The birds themselves may have sown these plants, since that process contributes to the colonization of pokeweed in disturbed and new areas. The egg shells were beautiful, some with a baby blue hue. The chicks in nests were distinctive in color, from the white of egrets to the black of glossy ibis. The colony of pokeweed was too dense to walk through in places, and we had to peek in and under to view low nests.

After the completion of the wading bird count, we prepared for the royal tern colony. Felicia oriented us to a different methodology for this egg count. Each member of the line had an eight-foot-long bamboo pole and would lay these down in front, creating a grid to walk through. Each person would have his or her own area to count. The shells lie directly on the soil and blend in, so great care must be taken to not step on them. At least one previous volunteer was careless in this delicate task. We needed to work quickly, since the adult birds would fly off as we began the survey, and if the nests were left unattended for too long, laughing gulls would fly in to make a meal of the unguarded eggs. Some sandwich tern eggs lay mixed in with the royals. With focus, we took on the first section, and when completed, we stood up and saw a ruptured egg, the product of a laughing gull raid. We then moved on and completed the royal tern colony survey. We continued to look for other wading bird nests and found none, until we reached the far end of the island.

After lunch, we moved to the next task for the day: putting up more "Closed Area" signs. We posted these all along the east beach. We completed a sample of pelican nests, looking to see how many eggs had fallen out of nests (zero). These tasks completed, we left the island for our next destination: the White Banks.

April 22, 2007

High tide 12:55 p.m. Predicted winds variable 5 knots, then SE 10–15 knots in the afternoon.

At midmorning, the magnificent atmospheric conditions make it an exquisite Sunday and Earth Day at the Romain Retreat landing. Still, a little wind would be nice, but it probably will not come up until later. Significant high tides have had an impact on the coast in the previous week, and farther north a northeaster created extensive flooding. Subsequently, the ramp is covered with one to two feet of dead cordgrass. I back *Kingfisher* down to the water. Snowbirds are cruising by, heading north, and as I jump on the hull to paddle out to the floating dock, I see a large yacht motoring by without slowing down. Noticing the large wake heading for the shallow water, I paddle briskly, making it over the crests before they break. The captain sees what he has done and motors down, but I am in no conciliatory mood. I stand up on deck to yell and wave my paddle at the offender. A little later in the marsh, my awareness registers that I have started the day in a funk.

We are heading across the ICW at 11:00 a.m. en route to the passage out Venning Creek. Past the shell rake along the ICW and into the channel behind, I will seek one of the smaller parallel creeks to Venning. Leaving the noise of the snowbirds and motorboats behind, we move slowly in the very light breeze. An oyster rock with shorebirds is a familiar benchmark. Since the tide is incoming, I use the paddle through this creek and then run aground with the crunching sound of daggerboard on oyster rock. We have found it in the center of this little creek! The water is clear enough to reveal the details of the oyster rock below the surface.

This one small oyster bar is a small tip of the iceberg constituting an important part of the refuge and the entire South Carolina coast—the Eastern or American oyster (*Crassotrea virginican*). This bivalve has extensive commercial value and provides gastronomical pleasure for natives and visitors alike. Partaking in oyster roasts is an important social and cultural ritual of the Lowcountry. The biology of the oysters offers more than their sedentary lives suggest. Oysters date back to the Triassic period (about 190 million years ago), and the genus *Crassostrea* dates to the Cretaceous period (about 135 million years ago). The oysters of this genus possess significant capabilities allowing distribution throughout the world: toleration of a range of salinities, turbidities, temperature and oxygen tension. They have freewheeling sexual lives, in which some members of a population switch from male to female or female to male. After fertilization in the water, the larval form of oysters, lasting from seven to ten days, have continued liberation as free swimmers. Their development includes a foot and gland needed for attaching to the substrate, whether a piling or other oysters. Metamorphosis continues after they attach. Their method for gaining nutrients—filter feeding—provides an important cleaning function for the waters.

Attaching to other oysters begins the development of the oyster reef, otherwise known as oyster bar or rock. The individual oysters generally are oriented vertically. The proximity to other oysters helps the fertilization process. The oyster reef is located throughout the refuge in the middle of the intertidal zone. The reef does not just include live oysters but also dead shells and a mix of mud and shells. The reef also provides habitat for a number of other marine animals that use the reef for protection, attachment and food. American oystercatchers, along with other animals, feed directly on the oysters themselves. Of the crustacean species, the oyster crab (*Pinnotheres ostreum*) has a slightly adverse effect on its host (inquilinism) and has only been found in South Carolina oysters 1 to 3 percent of the time. It is an occasional surprise for the oyster shucker, thought to impart good luck to the discoverer.

Pushing off, I continue paddling for propulsion, and the earlier rigging of the tiller extension aids in the technique. Arriving at a bend in the creek to the north, a view to the bay in the distance shows a little more wind. It is a long, straight stretch of light-wind sailing against some incoming tide. A johnboat floats at the mouth of the creek before the bay, and I recognize a couple of the neighborhood kids, Luke and Will, out fishing. Since I am

Marsh Island

heading as close to the wind as possible and not making the bay on this tack, I head past closehauled and paddle hard to enter the bay. We tack to get past the point and then come around for a long starboard tack. A little shoal reveals itself, with one-inch waves breaking, and so we make two more tacks to finally get in the clear. It is now a long starboard tack to windward across Bulls Bay for Marsh Island somewhere in the distance. The bay is void of other boats—I have miles of bay waters to myself. These waters are very smooth, but as we progress farther, the wind is incrementally strengthening, as if a volume control is gradually being turned up.

I brought along binoculars for locating Marsh Island and make it out to the east-northeast. In scanning the surface, a fin appears; it is not a dolphin but a shark. It is most likely a small fish, as looking through binoculars gives no scale to estimate size. In carrying along on this long point of sail, we encounter stakes at points in the bay. Shoals are off to starboard. I plan to take a turn around Marsh Island and decide to pass on the east side and round counterclockwise. I recall the shoals from my previous sail to this isle, and soon the daggerboard is hitting bottom. Small waves break on some shallows ahead, and we lose some windward gauge to go downwind of this shoal. I take a few peeks over with the binoculars at the island. I don't see the royal tern colony, but there is plenty of other bird activity.

We now squeeze up to make the southeast point and slide by in small swells without getting wet. More swells and shoals are ahead. In sailing into this area, a reef of mud sediments is observed under the water and just a few feet away. Quickly we tack, now heading directly against the oncoming small swells, and hold course just long enough to make the invisible lay line to get past the east side of the island. A quick tack back between swells and we are heading parallel to the east side beach. This side of the island is exposed to the swells coming from the Atlantic Ocean and continuing through Bulls Bay and is sharply eroded, with black sediments exposed across this beach. The deep channel on the north side is within reach, but the daggerboard still hits. While working hard to make this point, I view the congregation of birds arrayed on the land—an incredible sight.

We make the channel and bear off. Just off this beach is a group of sixty or seventy pelicans floating along, accompanied by some cormorants. As we sail closer, they all take off. About twenty feet off, we are paralleling the beach where my group landed the previous May for the DNR survey. Ahead is another grouping of pelicans and cormorants lined up along the shoreline.

Unlike a welcoming committee, they take off before our arrival, flying off in both directions away from *Kingfisher*. The shoreline ahead becomes salt marsh, as does much of the west side of the island. Before the marsh, a grouping of shorebirds stands alert, with willets and their smaller peers in attendance. They also take flight, peeling off on both sides of *Kingfisher*'s sail. At this corner of the island, we round up right around the marsh and up to a close reach, heading toward the west. I was concerned about water depth on this side, but we are fine. Passing the southwest corner, shrubs stick up and herons and egrets are on their nests.

We leave the island behind, and after one touch of the daggerboard we are heading back across the bay. The incremental rise of the wind continues, and the surface has a tiny chop. We are on a close reach to the southwest corner of the bay. This shallow body of water is wide open, with no boats around as we make this long port tack home. It is easy sailing, and there is just a little spray coming up onto the deck. The wind is very consistent, absent of puffs or changes in directions. I'm not sure how to account for this incredibly regular wind, but it makes for sublime sailing. We hold this port tack from Marsh Island to the mouth of Venning Creek, making it in just under an hour. We retrace the same passage through the narrow parallel branch of Venning and see the submerged oyster rock we crunched earlier now exposed in the air. We come up to closehauled to make it by, but no tacks are needed. The kids in the johnboat are now fishing just inside of the shell rake before the ICW when we pass. With one last miscalculation in passing over the point of this shell rake, I hit both the daggerboard and rudder. Without further ado, we cross the ICW, drop sail and coast into the landing.

WHITE BANKS

In the northeastern corner of Bulls Bay lies a series of little isles known as White Banks. As you approach them from the water, their whiteness is striking. The white is not sand but piles of shells, predominately oysters. The composition of shells resembles the shell rakes along the waterways. It seems these isles are built from the action of the waves of Bulls Bay piling up the shells over the years, particularly during storms. These islands have their sections of salt marsh, but shells are the predominate material. The material is also piled high in elevation, in places perhaps up to eight feet. The White Banks are a micro-archipelago unto themselves, with perhaps four main isles distinctive from other micro-isles.

Like Marsh Island, these isles are closed year-round due to seabird nesting. White Banks is a top site for oystercatcher nesting. Though not as isolated as Marsh Island, the White Banks are surrounded by the waters of Bulls Bay and are some distance from the mainland. Annually, DNR surveys the nesting on these islands. On the Marsh Island survey of May 18, 2006, I had the opportunity to walk on these isles and participate in the count.

After lunch, we left Marsh Island and headed northeast across the bay, soon spying the low, white blotches. Felicia Sanders, the leader of the survey, distinguished between West White Bank, Middle White Bank and East White Bank. We went around to the leeward side of West White Bank for our landing, pulling the Boston Whalers in through the marsh grass. For security, several of our party stayed with the boats while the

White Banks
May 26, 2007

McClellanville

Murphy Island

Cape Island

Alligator Creek

Cape Romain Harbor

Ramhorn Cr

Mill Cr

Mill Island

Slack Reach

Lighthouse Island

Casino Creek

Congaree Boat Creek

Horsehead Creek

Devils Den

Romain River

Muddy Bay

Skrine Creek

Dupre Creek

Jeremy Island

Intracoastal Waterway

Clubhouse Creek

Raccoon Creek

Key Inlet

Little Papas Creek

Nellie Creek

Papas Creek

Raccoon Key

Santee Path Creek

Key Creek

Jeremy Creek

Five Fathom Creek

Long Creek

Sett Creek

Bull River

White Banks

Sandy Point

N

Miles
0   1   2   3   4   5

rest waded through the marsh to the bank, composed predominately of solid oyster shells. A royal tern nesting colony lay ahead. The nesting area, like the island itself, was very narrow, and only three people across were needed. We made one counting set and then did one more across the shell ridge. To avoid the colony, we walked down the beach on the return to the boats. Always the beachcomber, I picked up an anomaly from the carpet of white shells: a half-round stone, cracked open. It appeared to be a flint. No one in the group was familiar with this artifact, and it was not until later that I connected it to an archaeological site in the Hobcaw area of Mount Pleasant. I had joined a group for the day as a volunteer back in the 1990s, when an archaeological team was investigating the site of the Rose shipyard at Hobcaw. Along with pipe stems, ceramics, glass and fasteners of wrought iron and brass, we found many of these flints in the sifting screen. They were brought over in ballast on ships and were used as gun flints. Perhaps a ship from the eighteenth century that desperately needed to make it to the Rose shipyard for repairs found its resting place in the shallow waters nearby and left a nugget for this twenty-first-century beachcomber to ponder.

We headed next to Middle White Bank, approaching from the west side. This was a more difficult landing, and we had trouble getting close to the beach. I tried to get out at one point, but the water level was too high. We finally made it to a better landing area. This isle was much larger than our first stop. Our survey area was also considerably larger and required a line of seven across. We needed to make three passes to survey the entire grid. The wildlife professionals worked to identify the eggs observed, which included gull-billed terns, Forster's terns and common terns. Several of the eggs also looked quite a bit like laughing gull eggs, requiring our experts to discriminate. Great care was needed on the survey and merely walking around, since the eggs blend in very well in this shell environment, rippled with ridges and valleys. I learned that the island, later in the season, would have a large nesting colony of black skimmers. Felicia has made it a point to not go on the island when eggs have hatched, having seen the frightened young birds walk right off into the water.

The survey came up with a limited number of eggs found. The calls of various terns were in the air, and the experts chatted about distinguishing one from another, the nuances that were beyond my perception. When our work was done, we departed the White Banks, heading north across this end of the bay before entering the shared mouth of Sett Creek and Bull River. Staying with Sett Creek, we reentered Five Fathom Creek for the familiar passage back to Jeremy Creek.

May 26, 2007

Low tide 11:00 a.m. Predicted winds E 5 knots in the morning, then SE 10–15 knots in the afternoon.

I launch *Kingfisher* at Jeremy Creek on a beautiful clear Saturday morning on Memorial Day weekend. I know to arrive at the landing early since it will fill up, and only a few spaces are open when *Kingfisher* goes in. While moving my car and trailer, I pass acquaintances Gene and Nancy Morrison putting in their seventeen-foot Cape Craft outboard. I hear Nancy comment about an anole on their boat right across from mine at the dock. It finds its way across the dock onto *Kingfisher*, taking up position on my bow. Gene is heading to an oyster rock to get bait and will wait on what the wind does before deciding where to fish. He thinks he might see me at Five Fathom Creek. He comments, in reference to reading my book *Exploring Bull Island*, "How many trips did you make out to Bull Island? If you had had an outboard and a four wheeler you could have done it in one day!" I laugh with him, say something about the importance of the journey versus the destination and bid him good luck on his fishing trip. As someone who rowed during his childhood and worked as a commercial fisherman, I can understand his preference for the efficient outboard. I have enjoyed the advantages of outboards myself. Yet sailing is more than just getting from point A to point B; it is a discipline, a passion, a challenge, an adventure, a way of living. Propelling oneself with only the action of the wind, currents and waves on sail and hull necessitates the learning and mastering of a complex skill set, even for the simple Sunfish. Sailing has made my life so much more stimulating and meaningful; it is hard to imagine its absence.

Heading out Jeremy Creek across the ICW to Town Creek, we are rolling with the outgoing tide to Five Fathom Creek. The reptile is still on the bow; I name him Gene's Lizard and sign him on as crew. I ponder that the anole, by osmosis in coming from Gene's craft, should bring me years of seamanship. No boats are around, and the east breeze makes for a fine reach, also confirming my plans to sail south rather than north toward Murphy Island. It is very clear air—a sky blue sky. A boat astern heads out Bull River, and ahead, above the marsh around the next bend, the Army Corps of Engineers' dredge *Try* is visible. In this section of creek we are beating to windward, and we make short tacks along the southwestern edge of the creek to give the large craft the full waterway. The *Try* has been working on keeping the channel open from the outlet into Bulls Bay and the ocean. Around the bend, a shrimp trawler appears in the distance, coming in from the bay, and when it finally passes it is revealed as *Miss Patience*, hailing from Bluffton, South Carolina. We make it out into the bay about 10:30 a.m. with the push of outgoing tide.

There is a little swell as I head almost west, paralleling the remnant of Sandy Point, now an island with shells piled up from storm waves. The front of the isle is hard mud sediments, looking like a rock jetty. The small swell of the bay is breaking over this island. Not far from here lies the location where Billy Baldwin lost his shrimp trawler, *Sherry Ann*, after running aground. Returning from a day of shrimp trawling long after sunset in rough weather, Baldwin lost his bearings and fetched up on the shoal. The southeast wind pounded the vessel that night. Not able to get off, or reach out for help, he and his crew spent the night on the wreck, alternately helpless and roaring drunk. They were on the roof of the cabin when help came. Baldwin shared with me that he never did like being out on the ocean and had other difficult experiences out there before this wreck. Baldwin finally gave up the bottle and the sea, turning to other pursuits, including an active career as a writer.

Past the point of what was Sandy Point, and beyond the old entrance to Five Fathom Creek with markers still pointing the way, we head to the north on our course to the White Banks. My crew, Gene's Lizard, has taken up a position on the mast just above the gooseneck, a definitely drier spot. He also is no longer green—he has turned to dark gray. With exploration around the White Banks the main plan, and with the restriction of staying on the water since all these islands are "Closed Areas" due to bird nesting, my course will depend on finding waterways providing *Kingfisher* with the ability to float. I will bank on the incoming tide for help in the afternoon.

Staying close to the northeast edge of the bay, I begin to look for a channel through the shoals revealed by small waves breaking outside of the most easterly of the White Banks. Later, I will look closely at the chart and notice that a small channel appears to lie along the edge, but in this

Pelicans roosting on remnants of Sandy Point in Bulls Bay.

moment we shape a course more to the west, looking for a channel and staying outside of the small break. A way appears ahead. Bearing off, we are ready to sail through when a small swell steeps up suddenly abeam. My reaction is too slow to bear off with it, and it breaks, throwing *Kingfisher* up on her beam ends. My movement is again too slow to scamper up to save the craft from capsize or to get over the side on the daggerboard for a quick righting, and suddenly I am spilled in the water to leeward. My feet find sandy bottom quickly—it is not even waist deep—and I work to scoop up gear tumbling from the cockpit. My untethered reading glasses have fallen from the deck and are sitting on the sail for my retrieval. I expect another wave, so without going around to the windward side, I grab the boom and mast and right the craft. I roll into the cockpit and get *Kingfisher* underway before another swell can have some more fun with us. The water in the cockpit is ankle deep, and luckily my sponge survived. Unfortunately, taking stock later, the missing includes a nice piece of braided mooring/tow line, another piece of strong webbing and two lighter webbings for securing the sail when lowered. I had about the same losses three years ago in my last capsize on a poorly executed jibe with my son Eliot onboard. Ironically,

White Banks

while chatting with another customer at the gas pump this morning, I was asked if it was hard to keep my boat upright. I knocked on a post (not hard enough), stating that it had been a few years. This experience today was the proverbial wake-up call.

After bailing out the boat and getting things shipshape, I notice that Gene's Lizard is still aboard but clinging for dear life to the halyard. He must have been thrown off the mast but found a lifeline. I have to jibe right away since this little channel heads back to the east between the shoals and a line of oyster reefs ahead. But we are inside the break and sailing past the easternmost of the White Banks. These small isles seem to have derived their name from the piles of shells exposed on a large portion of the isle, though salt marsh, oyster banks and tidal flats surround large portions. Getting around the back side of this isle, I notice that there is a small creek separating this isle from the next one. Hitting bottom often, I slowly make my way around, pulling the board up high and letting the wind float us downwind over shallower waters. A small shark, with dorsal fin and tail exposed, swims in these shallow waters (eight to ten inches deep). A small outboard in the distance comes roaring from the bay through that small creek, around the isle and back to the southeast toward Five Fathom Creek. We keep working to the west and look to pass on the inland side of the next of the White Banks. But the water continues to shoal and the way does not seem promising, with egrets walking and showing a lot of leg.

With the water getting shallower, I pull the daggerboard all the way out, allow the rudder to pop up out of the water and just drift with the sail flapping, occasionally using the paddle. Another small shark swims by astern. The bottom is soft, with mud underneath and grass growing abundantly. In several places in the shallows, a silent explosion off the bottom with plumes of mud suggests a disturbed stingray jetting off. It continues to get shallower as I head toward the west, and finally the hull meets up with the bottom. Ahead, the ripples of the water stop for a long, narrow area of slickness, and this is an exposed mud flat. The paddle will not advance me further here, so it is time to pull out lunch, relax and wait for the incoming tide. It seems that there is more water ahead; the dorsal fin of another small shark cruises by. I consider stepping out to drag the hull across the shoal, but the bottom is soft and I abandon this idea.

The hull finally starts slipping across the shoal, and now the paddle is creating some movement. We move a little farther, get a little rudder down and finally some sail trim. In the distance, I see a boat slowly moving past the last of the White Banks. I have entered a wide channel between two more of the banks and am able to push down the board and go to windward. What a sense of freedom! Ahead, I see the boat now crossing my bow and coming into the same waterway in which I am sailing. It is moving slowly, with two people moved to the bow and the engine tilted up to further reduce the draft. We continue on and tack back and forth with plenty of water. I am ready to head out to the bay and notice that the outboard astern has taken my earlier course, with the result that, even with all crew forward and the engine tilted up to the surface, they are aground. I take a close look at the isle to port (Middle White Bank) before bearing off and sailing west toward the last isle.

On the farthest west bank that I pass on the bayside, pelicans are on their nests. Other seabirds congregate here. Making it to the point, we round in for a look at the backside. The tentative plan has been to sail through here and north, then across to the entrance to Sett Creek, joining with Five Fathom Creek and the return to Jeremy Creek. But the waters of Bulls Bay, both in their freedom and beauty, are more inviting, and we turn and head back out into the bay. It is windward sailing, with shoals to avoid, but the wind is fair and the sea minimal. The first section between the shoals and the banks is not wide, but beyond there is plenty of room to sail. The conditions are sublime for this windward work, with the blues of sea and sky. The dark form of a dolphin appears off my bow, and though it doubles back to me, it does not rise again for a closer look. Approaching the old entrance to Five Fathom Creek, a quintet of pelicans crosses a medium distance overhead on its course for Marsh Island.

The incoming tide helps push us into the waterway behind the Sandy Point remnant. Gene's Lizard has regained the mast and looks cool and gray. The anole continues to advance up the mast until he finds the masthead and perches there. A shrimp trawler makes it into the creek from the bay before we get close. We pass two fishermen behind the Sandy Point remnant, with waves breaking over the narrow eastern point, and bear off with the tide to cruise back into Five Fathom Creek. We encounter dolphins near the western creek bank, but they keep their distance. The sail is quiet on the return, with only an occasional boat passing. Another trawler is also heading in, and I strive to push through Town Creek to avoid a passing in the narrow waterway. On a curve to starboard in which we hug the marsh, a red-tailed hawk flies off of a relocated cedar snag, lighting up the green marsh and

White Banks

Peregrine falcon in flight over the marshes of Five Fathom Creek. *Courtesy of Chris Snook.*

blue sky with its redness. The trawler is far astern when we make the ICW and sail across the waterway to the mouth of Jeremy Creek. In the distance it first appears like an anchored boat, then two and, when sailing by the raft, resolves into six craft anchored on the western side of the Jeremy Creek entrance. It is a full party, with blaring music and the howls and screams of the revelers. It appears like a warm-up for the Rockville Regatta party. The good news about this occurrence is that the noise is not out in the refuge, they are conserving fuel and the chance of impaired boating is reduced. And yes, it is Memorial Day weekend.

Swinging by and into the creek, I drop the sail before the dock, and we pass the final yards to the floating dock. After securing the boat and sail, I notice a now green anole on the aluminum dock. Like many crewmen who jump ship when land is reached, Gene's Lizard has survived the bay adventure. Mike and Ginny Prevost have just put in and come by to say hello. I also say hello to Billy Baldwin, who has just brought in his boat astern when dropping off a passenger. I speak with a fisherman, who asks if I was the sailboat out in Bulls Bay. He and his friend were fly fishing but were not able to get a fish on. He mentions that a charter captain had the same experience.

After pulling *Kingfisher* out, I see Gene Morrison come in. Speaking to him, I am not surprised to hear that he caught some fish, including a three-foot shark; additionally, he picked up a number of big jimmies. Before saying goodbye, I tell him to be on the lookout for his lizard. When we next meet, it appears that Gene's Lizard did find his way home, one mile down the road from the landing.

HAMMOCKS

B ehind the barriers islands, South Carolina has a collection of small islands classified as hammocks. By one DNR count, these isles number 3,467. Many are small: 53.7 percent are less than one acre, and 88 percent are less than ten acres. By definition, hammocks must be less than five hundred acres. Most of them are surrounded by salt marsh, hence the name "islands in the marsh." While the origin of the Sea Islands dates from the Pleistocene era, hammocks are from the Holocene era. A diverse array of habitats populates the hammocks, ranging from salt shrub to the mature live oak/palmetto/red bay maritime forest community. One hammock habitat is rare: the calcareous or high-calcium community, a product of the Native American deposition of shells in middens and mounds. The resulting high pH soil provides the environment for some rare plants, including smallflower mock buckthorn and Godfrey's swamp privet. Hammocks also provide habitat for a number of animals, with uses including refuge, nesting, feeding, mating and resting. They may be very important for some species in decline, including diamondback terrapins, diamondback rattlesnakes and painted buntings. Hammocks' mammal population includes deer, bobcat, otter, mink and raccoon.

The Cape Romain area has a collection of hammocks scattered throughout. A number of hammocks line the ICW and are the result of the deposition of dredge spoil through the digging of the waterway. A number of others are natural. Some are located next to other islands, like Lighthouse Island, and considered part of the larger island. Several are located near the

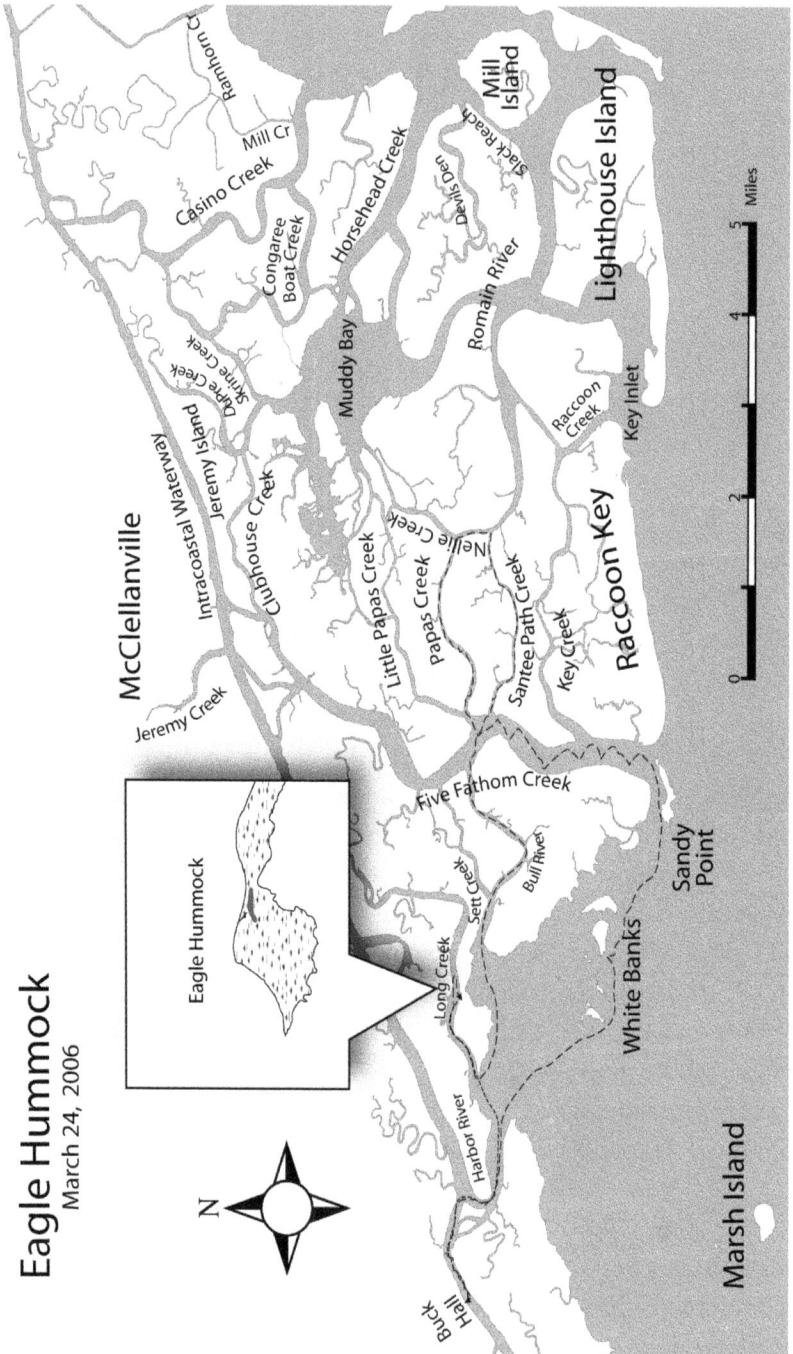

TRACING THE CAPE ROMAIN ARCHIPELAGO

Eagle Hummock
March 24, 2006

McClellanville

Ramhorn Cr
Mill Cr
Casino Creek
Congaree Boat Creek
Horsehead Creek
Mill Island
Devil's Den
Slack Reach
Lighthouse Island
Romain River
Muddy Bay
Cape Creek
Stripe Creek
Jeremy Island
Intracoastal Waterway
Clubhouse Creek
Little Papas Creek
Papas Creek
Nellie Creek
Santee Path Creek
Key Creek
Raccoon Creek
Key Inlet
Raccoon Key
Jeremy Creek
Eagle Hummock
Five Fathom Creek
Sett Creek
Bull River
Sandy Point
Long Creek
White Banks
Harbor River
Buck Hall
Marsh Island

Miles
0 2 4 5

N

bends of creeks. Few are named, though the loss of Native American names is quite possible. As I was drawn to all of the major islands in the Cape Romain area, I was also intrigued by these islands in the marsh, distinct because they rise above the surrounding cordgrass. Reaching them was an adventure in itself.

EAGLE HUMMOCK

No chart or map I have seen has this little hammock identified as Eagle Hummock. The NOAA chart labels this area of marsh "Morants Point." Visible from all around the many nearby waterways, the palmettos and cedars stand up prominently, marking this spot at the northeastern end of Bulls Bay. It is a little hammock—a sliver of elevation running northeast-southwest, perhaps eight yards wide for a good bit of its length. This spot was distinctive enough to be identified as the easternmost point of a king's land grant to the Morrison family. It must have had a tree that was a favorite roost for eagles, just as now there is an eagle that roosts in a tree on a hammock along Clubhouse Creek.

Eagle Hummock figures prominently in the Archibald Rutledge poem "Ghost Point." As the hammock is a landmark for boaters in the great sea of marsh, much like the distant lighthouses, its repetition in the first line of each stanza of the poem provides a geographic and poetic reference:

> *Eagle Hummock lies behind*
> *And the broad bay lies before:*
> *Between the bay and the open sea*
> *Are sunken reefs of treachery*
> *And ships that sail no more.*

> *Eagle Hummock, where always*
> *The storm-bent cedars sigh:*
> *Gazing out over the foaming tracts*
> *To the surf-line's glimmering cataracts*
> *Where wrecks and perils lie.*

Eagle Hummock lies behind
And Harbor Creek before:
Beyond is the bay and the Light House far,
Where the brave and lonely keepers are
At watch on the lonely shore.

Eagle Hummock—there at night
When stars with storms are red,
With the dim sea moaning far away,
With a sound unheard by men, the bay
Give up her wandering dead.

Eagle Hummock lies behind
Where the drowned men come on shore:
And save for the obscure laughter heard,
Silently—save for the grey mist stirred
By them who sail no more.

MARCH 24, 2006

Low tide 9:17 a.m. Predicted winds NNW 8–16 knots.

The morning is cold and raw at Buck Hall landing, and the high temperatures are projected to be fifteen degrees below average. The previous night saw considerable rain, and dampness lingers. With the continued closure of the Ashley Landing at Jeremy Creek in early 2006, this landing will today provide my access to Bulls Bay and some of the islands of the Cape Romain archipelago. The Buck Hall landing is virtually deserted; there is only one truck and trailer in the lot. I have donned layers of clothing, foul weather gear on the outside and a beanie on my head for good measure. Prior to hoisting sail, another truck pulls up to drop in a weathered craft. We exchange greetings, and the chilly weather provides a shared subject.

I am off and beating to the northeast up the ICW. The wind is patchy due to the shore blanket from the mainland at the Shellmore community. The shoreline here is built up with bulkheads, riprap and tall houses. A blue snowbird trawler is heading north, too, and I give him the channel. After a couple of tacks, we bear off toward the east in the ICW channel. We pass two smaller creek mouths, heading on to the larger entrance to Harbor River that leads to the northern end of Bulls Bay. The course is now broad reaching and running with the wind, and the falling tide is also adding a push. There is only one other boat, a crabber, in the vicinity. I look to the east to identify the creek mouth I will utilize on my return trip. In the opening of the creek into the bay, I am startled by a marine body close aboard to starboard and a loud exhalation. Other dolphins also gambol with *Kingfisher*.

The dolphin's ability to navigate in these often murky and shallow waters, clearly understanding the long passages through tidal channels, is remarkable. This skill appears to be the result of a highly developed production and hearing of sounds. The sonic emission capability takes place through the delphinid use of echolocation, enabling these mammals to survey their environment, including the location of prey. Some of the specialized acoustic mechanisms of dolphins are the melon, where the clicks of echolocation are emitted, and the lower jaws, where the echoes are received and transmitted through lipid fat channels to the ear bones. This information is then forwarded to the impressive dolphin brain, which is larger than the human brain.

I had the opportunity one windy February morning on Bull Island to dig out of the beach sands the large skull of a bottlenose dolphin. The size of the cranial cavity was most impressive. The debates about dolphin intelligence are long standing and controversial, but clearly an advanced capability of the dolphin brain is auditory-spatial memory. Using our human imagination, we can conceive of the dolphin having rich sonic maps, containing information about water depth, prey locations and passages through the extensive waterway systems of the Cape Romain archipelago. I must admit that my mind has had difficulty comprehending the sonic capability of these familiar marine mammals.

We are broad reaching now out to the White Banks. To the southwest, huge mud flats are exposed, littered with derelict crab pots as if they were a crop ripe for harvest. The next startle comes with a long bang; a hard collision with something fixed underwater—an old piling perhaps? I recall seeing a jagged piling sticking up out of the water as I planed through the area on my first sail out of Buck Hall in May 2005. I'm hoping the collision is not with my hull, and a check of my daggerboard reveals the impact on the mahogany: a large gash three inches from the bottom of the board. I steer toward a line of crab-trap buoys and closer to the nearest of the White Banks. There is some elevation to this shell-covered isle.

As I prepare to round this southernmost of the White Banks, I recall again my sail from last year. Our present location is the spot where I turned around. It was the weekend of the Shrimp Festival in McClellanville, and boaters returning from that location up the ICW to the north found that they were facing a strong southwest breeze, providing for a cooler and wetter trip than earlier in the day. I found myself with increasing wind, inadequate clothes and a lack of knowledge of the waters. I viewed the scene and contemplated bearing off into an area with numerous exposed obstructions, remnants from Hurricane Hugo, and unknown shoals and oyster reefs. With both prudence and regret, I returned back to Buck Hall, awaiting this day to cross the northern section of Bulls Bay to Sandy Point.

The breeze is moderate, with the wind's direction allowing a close reach in the lee of the White Banks for the crossing. Once again, the path marked by crab buoys is helpful in the navigation of these shoal waters. To the south, channel markers made of tall pilings stand in the distance, along with, closer, half-submerged wooden structures. After passing two more of the White Banks, there are some lower marsh isles and oyster banks to port. *Kingfisher* has plenty of water, and after passing another bank, a small creek opens between an oyster reef and a taller shell bank. I round-up to explore, going to windward into this small waterway. Small waves created by *Kingfisher*'s wake to leeward break over an oyster bar. We hit bottom and tack, and soon, off to starboard, hit bottom again. We sail a little farther, then tack and luff, noticing oystercatchers on the shell bank. I would like to explore further but instead head back out into the bay, continuing the crossing toward Sandy Point.

The whiteness of Sandy Point appears ahead, but beyond is a shape not immediately recognizable. It is some marine machine, with an unusually curved boom projecting into the air, located behind the approaching isle. Markers line the channel, but I am somewhat confused. A sandy beach is ahead, but I do not see the cross on the point observed in January. Upon closer approach, the mysteries are solved. I have located the "real" Sandy Point, a small isle that "calved off" from Raccoon Key when Five Fathom Creek found a new inlet into the bay. My landing in January was on the "new" Sandy Point, on the west end of Raccoon Key. These details are newer than my NOAA chart, but a look at a more current satellite image reveals the reality and the startling dynamics of this area.

The remains of this barrier island once part of Raccoon Key is a proper setting for discussing climate change and the future of this section of the coast. Sea level rise is a reality, and predictions about its impact are percolating along the East Coast. A report from the 1990s suggested that by the year 2100, the marshlands and barrier islands in Cape Romain National Wildlife Refuge will have shrunk by 58 percent. A study published in 2008 gave further predictions, looking at various scenarios correlated with the range of sea level rise projected by the International Panel on Climate Change: between thirty and one hundred centimeters by 2100. Three scenarios were modeled on increases of thirty-nine, sixty-nine and one hundred centimeters by 2100. Using the area of salt marsh as a benchmark, the predictions for percent loss by 2100 would be 47, 83 and 95 percent. Even in the conservative prediction, the loss of salt marsh, the nursery of the coastal zone, would be severely impacted, and in the worst scenario, the result for the ecosystem would be catastrophic. In terms of undeveloped dry land, the reduction in the three scenarios would be 27, 52 and 69 percent. As Sandy Point has disappeared, the other barrier islands would also shrink. One veteran observer of the refuge, longtime commercial fisherman Ervin Ashley, remarked that he anticipated one day in the near future when there would be open water between Cape Island and the mainland.

Sailing into Five Fathom Creek we are greeted by a dolphin. There is a clear view of the dredge working off in the distance in the channel now used by shrimp trawlers. The "curve" of the boom is actually the discharge of sediment and seawater in the area away from the channel. I do recall the isle behind me from my trip in January, with its point on Five Fathom Creek across from Raccoon Key covered with birds. USFWS signs along this isle indicate that it is closed, and on my quick stop I stay on the beach. Oystercatchers walk on the isle's flat, and there are higher shell piles to the east.

As we sail by the point of this isle, I ease sail and stall to watch the birds. A swell from the ocean comes in this inlet, and *Kingfisher* easily rises over the crests. The black, chiseled point of mud sediments accommodates pelicans, cormorants and gulls, whose consorts rest on the far side of the inlet. The swell is breaking on this bird-covered point, shooting spray into the air and creating a classic maritime scene. In the background, the dredge is spewing black sediment.

I sheet in, and we begin the beat up Five Fathom Creek. The wind is a steady ten knots from the north, and the tide is pushing *Kingfisher* along on the beat to windward. The smooth water makes for fine sailing, with plenty of sea room between the banks. The bank of the marsh on the west is mainly black mud with fissures carved into the *Spartina* and filled with shells deposited in the gaps. The sun is appearing for the first time today, and a magical image appears about a mile astern—a sun shaft lights up the black point of the isle, and the spray tossed high is bathed in this light. The creek presents an array of bird life: a quartet of oystercatchers beating south, a group of cormorants crossing to the west and a trio of pelicans cruising the surface along our course to windward.

We are already past the Key Creek entrance to the east and then pass the entrance to the Santee Path Creek. Across the creek is the opening to Bull River, my planned return passage to the bay and Buck Hall. However, it is early, and with the wind solid and the weather improving, I ignore damp and cold feet (despite wet suit socks) and plan an eastward voyage through Papas Creek, south on Nellie Creek and then a return on Santee Path Creek, an essential circumnavigation of the encircled large marsh island.

Papas Creek is fairly wide, perhaps fifty yards. There is a gentle bend, and several tacks are needed on a northern turn. The creek, banks and marsh present a constant façade without variation. A procession of crab buoys points the way, and there are no side branches confusing the course. The sky continues to clear, and the breeze remains steady. Red-winged blackbirds make their presence known. We turn to the southeast now, and the tallest Cape Romain lighthouse is directly ahead in the distance. Making Nellie Creek, we bear off to run with the wind. It is a good time to pull out lunch. The sun is coming out fully as the clouds of the front push offshore. Remaining are the blue sky, a smattering of white, fair-weather cumulus clouds and the steady breeze.

We jibe into the opening to the Santee Path Creek and begin the reach to the west. There is little incoming flow in this creek, about one-half the width of Papas Creek. A similar uniformity of width and creek banks prevails. Standing up in *Kingfisher*'s cockpit, I see the marsh grass stretching out as far as my eye permits. This waterway seems to exist for the passage of small craft, unless a stop is needed to pull up a crab trap. *Kingfisher* makes steady progress until the final section, where the creek turns northwest prior to connecting to Five Fathom Creek. Progress slows as we tack in the narrow creek. Soon, the circumnavigation of this unnamed marsh island is complete as we head into Five Fathom Creek again. This circled marsh island was one of John Bowman's, labeled #2. It is fine windward sailing, and we shortly reach the opening to Bull River, my westward passage to Bulls Bay. We reach off into this creek and find on crab-trap buoys a good incoming flow with *Kingfisher*. I finish lunch on the broad reach through this delightful waterway.

We soon pass the confluence with Sett Creek on the north side of Bull River. Sandwich terns are fishing as the creek opens up into the bay. Bull River parallels Long Creek and farther north, the ICW, identified by the masts of snowbirds heading north. Off to starboard a hammock arises out of the marsh in an area known as Morants Point on the chart, but to locals it is known as Eagle Hummock. It sits on the marsh peninsula between the northern reach of the bay and Long Creek. Exploring near the marsh edge, there are no creeks appearing to access the hammock, only marsh and oyster beds. We continue on, staying close to the point, and I decide to head up into Long Creek to explore this side of the hammock. A group of gray shorebirds takes off from the point as we tack by.

We sail into this creek a little and, after turning to head back, abruptly turn once again to go a little farther. Around a slight bend to the east, the hammock is closer to the bank. I look for any little creek into the marsh, but the only waterway seen is gator-sized. Reaching the bend, I tack and head back toward the bay. Spontaneously, I turn again, heading upwind, drop sail and paddle to the tiny creeklet. Missing the opening, I have to paddle a little upwind before squeezing in, literally, with each side of *Kingfisher*'s beam touching marsh grass. Paddling through this little crease in the marsh only gets us about two-thirds of the way to the hammock before *Kingfisher* runs out of water. The tide is still incoming, but it will be awhile before the hull will have enough water to make the hammock. I've gotten this far, so surrendering to the marsh, I step out, securing *Kingfisher* with my paddle shoved into the mud and the bowline fastened. Wet suit socks and sandals protect my feet from the oysters underfoot.

It is a short walk to this hammock, a narrow ridge about eight yards wide and eighty yards long. There is a large stand of yaupon holly with a few mature palmettos providing a picturesque profile. The top of the ridge is covered with dead cordgrass and a smattering of plastic bottles, indicating that the highest tides cover this "high ground." A hackberry tree with roots exposed and new yellow foliage sits on the edge, dividing marsh from hammock. The hammock runs on an east–west axis, with the east end marked by a live cedar with several large, dead, bleached cedars nearby. Whether this isle in the marsh is in the making or in decline is not clear—it seems both tentative and tenacious. It does not surprise me that Archibald Rutledge used it as a subject in his poem "Ghost Point."

On the walk back to *Kingfisher*, I use a derelict shrimp baiting pole to keep from sinking in the mud. Sitting on the bow, I note that both *Kingfisher* and I are a mess. I take off my sandals, tie them on the bow and begin to paddle out, stern first. Once making Long Creek, I turn *Kingfisher* and paddle up wind for the raising of sail. The effort is clumsy, and we're soon almost back in the marsh, running aground. While pulling up the board and tacking, both my winter beanie and my bamboo hiking stick secured to the boom fall into the water at once. I grab the beanie before it sinks, but I'm not fast enough to grab the stick before it is out of reach. A quick tack has us headed back, but the tide has pushed me downwind and I miss the stick. On the second attempt, I head right to the grass, round into the wind on the marsh's edge, retrieve the stick and tack out. This adventure over, it is easy sailing now back out to the bay and the entrance to Harbor River and the ICW.

Once in the ICW, the masts of snowbirds are visible, but closer is a white, sixty-foot yacht heading north, the first craft I've seen since the crabber in the bay this morning. The skipper has throttled low as we pass, and *My Boat* begins to kick up a substantial wake as he works to get his craft up to speed. The wind becomes sketchy with the mainland shore blanket, and tacks are required to make it around the point to head southwest in the ICW. A loud noise from a little outboard is coming from the vicinity of Buck Hall ahead. After landing, I learn from another boater that this is a racing outboard, and we watch as the racer makes passes in the protected waters of the ICW. In talking with this racing outboarder after he returns to the landing, I learn that he hits speeds up to sixty miles per hour and the only thing that keeps him from running faster is "fear." These outboarders are interested in my little sailing craft and wonder what happens with waves and flipping over. I explain that this craft can manage waves well, even outside, but I am careful about when to head out to the ocean. The outboarders are from Aynor and are camping at Buck Hall. Their preacher is leading a revival in Walterboro, and they have brought their boats along for their marine and religious experiences in the Lowcountry. I wish them well as I take my leave.

MIDDLE BULLS BAY HAMMOCKS

This narrow band of hammocks in the middle of the interior of Bulls Bay on the edge of the extensive marshland appears an artifact of this shallow body of water. Similar islands elsewhere have been described by geologists as naturally formed by the action of a previously existing inlet located toward the ocean. The inlet's waves would have deposited sand on the marsh, and the later migration of the inlet would have left the higher ground ripe for botanical colonization. Though the geological history of Bulls Bay is not definitively documented, it is felt that the Santee River once discharged here; the location of these hammocks parallel to the shoreline and midway between the barrier islands is a tantalizing clue.

The cedar and salt-shrub community dominates these hammocks. Another botanical community exists in the border between the *Spartina* salt marsh and the hammock's upland: the salt flat. These distinct high marsh communities exist throughout the Cape Romain area. The salt flat is a high

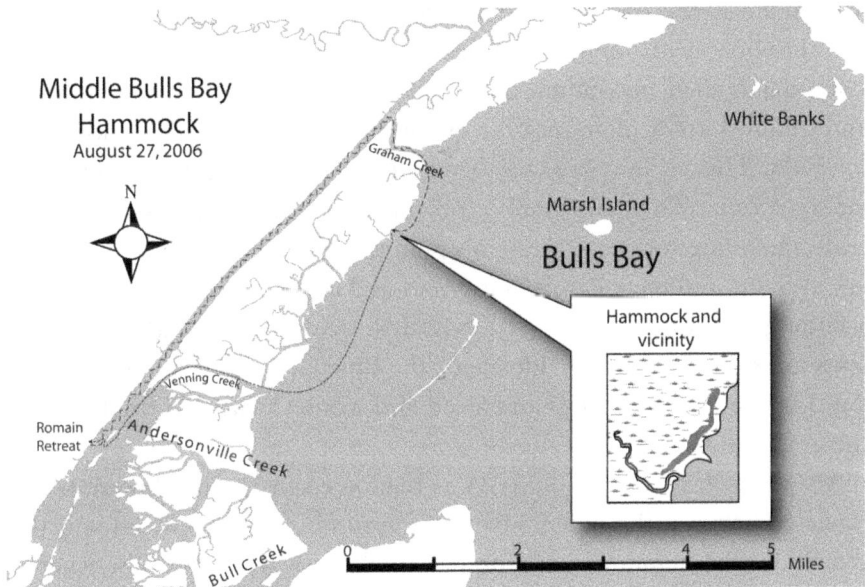

Middle Bulls Bay
Hammock
August 27, 2006

N

Graham Creek

White Banks

Marsh Island

Bulls Bay

Hammock and
vicinity

Venning Creek

Romain
Retreat

Andersonville Creek

Bull Creek

0   2   4   5   Miles

saline environment of the high salt marsh, and in areas along this hammock the salt flats are devoid of vegetation. Yet in other areas of the flats, two main groups of plants are able to colonize this area: the succulents (here glasswort and saltwort) and salt grass. The locations of colonies of glasswort became a marker for *Kingfisher* landings along the salt marsh with the anticipation of solid footing.

August 27, 2006

High tide 10:30 a.m. Predicted winds E 10 knots.

The resident kingfisher sounds its presence as I drop *Kingfisher* off the trailer in early morning at the Romain Retreat landing. We are off at 8:15 a.m. and tacking north up the ICW in light winds. Setting a course out of the entrance to Venning Creek is a consideration for the trip to the hammocks in the marsh midway up Bulls Bay, but I choose to sail up the ICW, with plenty of water depth going to windward. These hammocks have been on my mind for sometime. They stand out in the distance from the vantage point of the pier head at Romain Retreat and in the past appeared as if the vegetation projecting above the surrounding marsh was a schooner rig.

We are tacking into north-northeast winds, passing the waterway homes of Romain Retreat and finding the winds picking up a little. Fortunately, no other boat traffic appears on this Sunday morning, keeping the water smooth and all of my options open. The sound of a motor becomes loud, and finally I see a plane not far overhead roar past us going north up the ICW. This yellow plane has been a familiar sight in the Lowcountry for some time. We pass a pier with commercial craft and several derelict craft, including trawlers rotting away in the marsh. Other winged flyers are also out in force—egrets, ibis, terns and a great blue heron. We pass a large grassy area, the Sewee Coastal Retreat Center. Blue and green tents are still standing as evidence of the Blue Crab Festival the previous day. Light green port-a-lets and a red and white Coca-Cola truck accent the green grass.

My decision to stay in the ICW is reinforced by the fair breeze being funneled between the banks—the high ground of the mainland and the growth on the hammocks and dredge spoil on the bay side. The wind is unsullied and allows for a wonderful moving meditation in "climbing the wind." We are climbing well, and these moments sailing to windward are as special as the destination. To the north, the yellow plane is playing in the clear, open skies and sculpting tight banks in the air. It finally returns and passes directly overhead; a wave of my hat is perhaps returned with a wave of its wings. The airfoil of its wings and resulting lift in the air are a key to my climbing the wind: the airfoil of *Kingfisher*'s sail allows the wind to flow around and provide lift, pushing us to within forty-five degrees of the wind direction.

This sailing to windward also illustrates the psychological concept of flow. For the beginning sailor, getting the boat from point A to a point B directly upwind provides the biggest challenge and frustration. It demands a certain level of skill to progress into the wind, requiring not just sail trim and controlling the heading of the boat but also the acquisition of the feel for the boat through the sailor's hand on the tiller. Course changes become intuitive and necessary in responding to every little nuance and variance of wind direction and speed, with corresponding adjustments in hull and sail trim. The interaction between the degree of challenge of the conditions and the level of skill of the sailor becomes the catalyst for the flow experience, where the sailor becomes totally focused, moves to a higher level of perception, is more completely in the moment, loses track of time and further develops a passion for the pursuit. The flow I experience in this moment is matched by the flow around *Kingfisher*'s sail, taking us farther to the north.

We pass a tall white house with three stories, where a kingfisher leaves his perch to rattle. The ICW is long and straight in this section, requiring no markers. The wind continues to come right down the pipe, meeting no obstructions from the shorelines, but does shift to the east around the community Bulls Bay Overlook. The bulkhead of its marina appears only good for laughing gulls to perch on. Ahead a stretch of undeveloped shoreline precedes the Seewee Shell Ring. A small creek winds into the marsh and at this tide would allow *Kingfisher* to slip in all the way to the ring. On the other side, a high bank of dredge spoil has replaced the natural hammocks and sports some different vegetation by opportunistic colonizers. The spoil bank also closes off views to the bay. Sailing along a little farther to the north allows some views out to the bay and the hammocks on the edge of the bay in the distance.

A red can in the ICW marks the location of the entrance to Graham Creek. I gladly bear off and head out on a reach against the still incoming tide. The view is of a wide world now: marsh and bay to the east. The sky is blue and accented with fair-weather cumulus clouds. The hammocks appear to the south. The creek turns to the east, and we are now beating again to windward. The current is still strong, and we slip to leeward on the starboard tack in cutting across the flow. We continue tacking to and fro and finally, on port tack, clear a point in the marsh to the south, allowing entrance to the bay.

The large, shallow bay is sparkling with brightness. In the distance is the low outline of Marsh Island. I consider sailing up and around this isle, but I decide to save energy for the hammock exploration. Some unusual handmade markers off to port have an ambiguous meaning, but the bay on this tide has plenty of water for *Kingfisher*. We ease off in reaching around toward the hammocks, and I wonder if there will be an access to the high ground through the marsh. Out on the bay, the marsh appears extensive. As we approach the northeast end of the hammock, a tiny creek appears but will require an entrance through the marsh grass. We continue the search downwind, heading to the southwest and looking for a more encouraging entrance. No promising landing spots present themselves in the midsection of the wide marsh adjoining the hammock, so we continue to sail. An object with a red roof sits on the hammock in the distance, and I speculate that it is a Hurricane Hugo remnant beached here. The daggerboard is doing its usual duty as depth finder, and a solid hit on an oyster reef scares me off from staying too close to the marsh.

Toward the southwest end of the main hammock a creek appears with some width, and we head straight in here toward the hammock. Without hesitation, I jibe into the creek and feel with the board for the bottom. A sharp turn appears ahead to the south, and then the creek stays parallel to the hammock. The creek continues and curves away from the high ground, so I tack and head to the marsh closest to the hammock. I pull up the board, and we sail into the grass until we are stopped. The grass is tall, and the water is still of some depth. I'm ready to muck through, but before making the plunge I stand up on the deck to survey the area for better landings. Back toward the first curve in the creek there is a different color green that is a break in the *Spartina*, and it has the look of an area covered with glasswort. Through experience, I have found these glasswort colonies to be a good indication of more solid ground. I extract *Kingfisher* from the marsh with paddle strokes, giving me sternway, and head to the place of glassworts. This place is better than anticipated for a landing. I pull up *Kingfisher*, leaving the sail up and tie her off to the paddle rammed into the mud.

The walk is easy across the flat of mud and glassworts. The edge of the marsh and hammock is a natural place to walk. My time for exploration is limited due to the outgoing tide. The walk includes going to the southern end and around to the west side. No sign of shell midden is evident on these hammocks. An animal path extends away from the south end toward the next hammock, but it is time to rig up and beat out while the tide allows. The creek is very narrow, requiring quick tacks, but with plenty of water we are easily out into the bay. Two other islets sit to the east, but they are just marsh at this tide. I come off to a heading to the south-southwest.

We are running down the bay, and the small waves and bright sun create a sparkling surface. On our course down the bay I intend to make a stop at Bird Bank. I follow the chart for a while but realize this isle is no longer at that location. Later, I process that this isle is more of a shoal in its present state since it is underwater at this tide. A reach across to Bull Island would be easy, but we continue to run off and enjoy the freedom of plenty of water. Ahead, sun reflects on sand in the distance. We continue to run on but see ahead that the "sand islets" are sand and shell on the southern edge of the bay. Waves are lumping up more, and the effect of the outgoing tide opposed to the wind is apparent. This wave action is also a sign of Venning Creek, and seeing the mouth in the marsh, I jibe to head in. We surf a few waves on the ride into the creek.

I round up in the inside sheltered waters and jump in with a good hold on the hull to cool off. Back in *Kingfisher*, I run off through the creek, and the solid breeze makes it easy to overcome the outgoing tide. I pull out my lunch on the easy point of sail. The creek eventually curves to the southwest and continues beyond the shell rakes separating this little waterway from the ICW. Coming back from the creeks and bay where I encountered virtually no other craft, the solitude and wilderness of the bay ends quickly with the commotion of the boat traffic in the waterway ahead.

We pass several channels leading out to the landing and the ICW but carry on to the entrance to Anderson Creek. Stretching the sail out, I am rewarded with an array of natural wonders: an osprey overhead, dolphins in Anderson Creek and finally a loggerhead just off to starboard, gasping for a breath. I follow the dolphins along the shallows to starboard, attracted by the wildlife right across from my landing. A shell rake lies ahead, covered with oystercatchers. I let the sail go and draw closer, as quietly as possible, but they take alarm and fly off. A couple of terns stay, and while taking some photos, my bow comes to rest on the shell rake. Pulling off, I head into the dock, beyond which wood storks are circling over the freshwater impoundment. After landing and pulling *Kingfisher* out, I grab water and the remainder of my lunch to go back out on the dock for a last look. The water, marsh and sky provide a wonderful visual feast. One final reward appears: a pair of kingfishers in raucous interaction. They carry on for a while as I linger.

BULLS BAY

The string of barrier islands between Charleston and Georgetown is broken for a seven-mile section within Cape Romain National Wildlife Refuge. At the line of the barrier islands, this break in the coastal strand is defined by the Northeast Point of Bull Island to the southwest and Sandy Point to the northeast. The shallow body of water in this opening is called Bulls Bay. Before its name was changed in historical times, these waters were Seewee Bay, a name derived from the Native Americans residing in this area.

The presence of this open section of the coast has generated speculation on its origins. One hypothesis by Miles and Michel suggests that the bay is a relict of a valley dug out by a piedmont river during one of the glaciations (Kansan or Illinois). The river was most likely an ancient track of the present Santee River. Interestingly, a large area of sand, described as an old delta lobe, lies on the continental shelf off Bulls Bay. This abundance of sand is considered the possible source for the barrier islands to the southwest.

Bulls Bay occupies a large amount of surface area, roughly half of CRNWR's sixty-four thousand acres. In contrast to the extensive surface waters, the lack of depth is significant, and certainly both an impediment and a hazard to navigation. The NOAA navigation chart "Winyah Bay Entrance to Isle of Palms" displays soundings in feet for the bay, and "1" appears more than any other sounding. Tradition suggests that, in

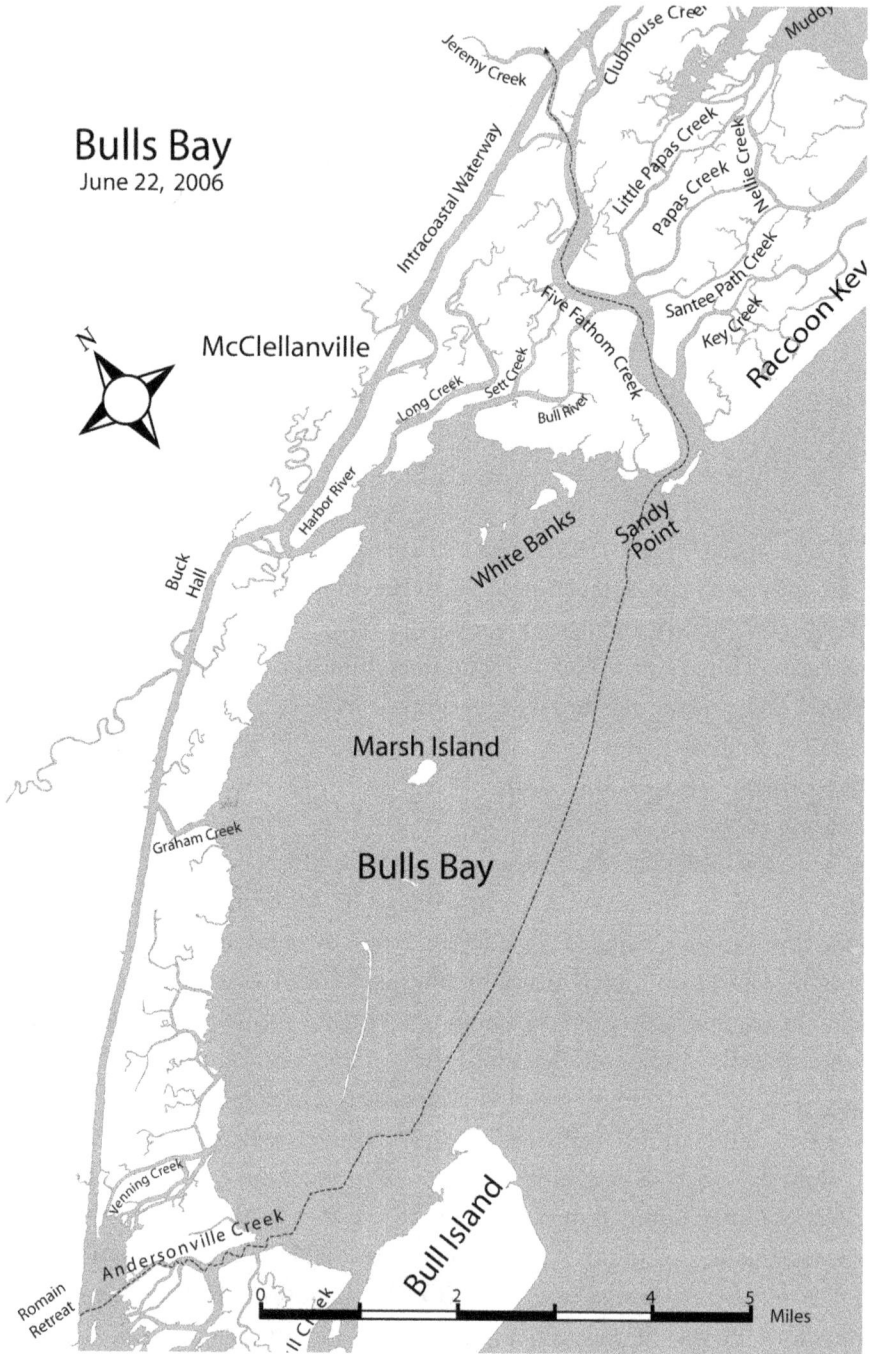

Bulls Bay
June 22, 2006

N

McClellanville

Jeremy Creek

Clubhouse Cree·

Muda·

Intracoastal Waterway

Little Papas Creek

Papas Creek

Nellie Creek

Five Fathom Creek

Santee Path Creek

Key Creek

Raccoon Key

Long Creek

Sett Creek

Bull River

Harbor River

White Banks

Sandy Point

Buck Hall

Marsh Island

Graham Creek

Bulls Bay

Venning Creek

Andersonville Creek

Bull Island

Romain Retreat

0   2   4   5   Miles

the past, locals would move the rudimentary navigation markers from the known channels, and when nonlocal boaters would run aground, the locals would come to their rescue—for a fee. Another story adding to the legendary shallowness of these waters relates the request by a nonnative boater to a local for guidance in finding more water for a passage. The local replied, "There is plenty of water everywhere—it is just spread out real thin."

Bulls Bay has certainly not been a safe harbor for offshore vessels. Each end of the bay has provided for protected and deep anchorages: Five Fathom Creek to the north and Bull Creek to the south. An excellent firsthand account from the southern anchorage exists for one of the most deadly hurricanes in the annals of the Lowcountry. The vessels in the Bull Creek anchorage on September 27, 1822, were in for a night of survival. The United States revenue schooner *Gallatin* rode out the Great Gale of 1822 nearby in the lee of the island. The following is an extract from the log of the *Gallatin*:

> *Friday Evening, Sept. 27ᵗʰ—At 10 o'clock, commenced raining, with fresh breezes—at 11, called all hands to send down yards and topmasts; succeeded in getting down the fore yard and housing the main top mast, but in the act of getting the main top sail yard on deck, a whirl of wind snapped the fore top mast short off by the cap; the wreck of the fore top mast and fore top sail yard hung in the rigging for about 25 minutes, when the fore top sail, (a new sail) blew from the yard and went in ribbons, wind at this time S.W.—The wreck was clearing in the course of an hour, but the wind had now increased to a perfect hurricane, the sea making a perfect breach fore and aft: and no one could get from one end of the vessel to the other without crawling— About half past 1 A.M. began to drag, although there were three anchors ahead, (the best bower having been let go at the commencement of the blow) and nearly a whole cable veered away on each—At 2, she struck on an oyster bank, where, after splitting open the head of the rudder, she brought up. Suddenly the wind, which was now at South, died away, and it remained calm for about 10 minutes—It then shifted to S.W. and instantly began to roar with full as much, if not more violence than before—This brought the vessel across the tide, and one hand was stationed at each mast with an axe ready to cut away—she*

was several times nearly on her beam ends, but righted so quick as to induce us to save the masts—She finally swung round along side of the marsh, which then began to appear, from the tides falling as rapidly as it had risen—we then lay comparatively safe—At 4 A.M. the gale moderated, but left us ashore very high up alongside the marsh—At day-light, discovered several vessels ashore in the marsh, some distance from us—On examination, found we had lost the following articles, vis—One new fore top sail blown away; fore top mast gone, most of the rigging carried away; for top sail yard, and larboard yard arm carried away—The launch parted a four inch rope, and was lost; the other cutter much damaged, although hoisted in; top gallant sail split to pieces; main sail and fore sail split to pieces, although laying on deck; several spars blown over board; some running rigging cut and carried away; main top mast and top gallant stay both gone, &c—Whilst laying along side of the marsh, a boat called the Favorite of Columbia, after drifting over a large island of marsh, which was then covered by the tide, passed close by the cutter; the people on board her screaming for assistance; but could render them none—providentially their anchor shortly afterwards took a fresh hold, and she rode out the remainder of the storm, loosing part of her deck load, rudder, oars and camboose, and her sail torn.

Bull's Island was cut entirely through by the sea, at the S.W. end, and three houses blown down, some stock drowned, &c.

The *Charleston Courier* later reported that one man onboard was seriously injured by hailstones.

Another mariner found safe harbor on the opposite end of the bay later that century. Nathaniel Bishop, rowing south on his two-thousand-mile voyage in his paper canoe, was out in Bulls Bay at dusk and looking for a place to camp for the night. He was in an anxious situation in the growing dark, navigating between the hazards of the breakers on Raccoon Key, the "old disturbers of my peace"—dolphins—and the sharp raccoon oysters of the shoal waters. With the mainland off in the distance, Bishop found relief when he spied tall schooner masts of a vessel anchored in protected waters, Five Fathom Creek. He entered the creek mouth and was offered the services of a U.S. navy vessel, the coast survey schooner *Caswell*. He spent the night in a stateroom on this ship before leaving the next day for his row across Bulls Bay.

Bulls Bay

The bay is edged by salt marsh on the inshore side. The NOAA chart mentioned above has at least half of the area marked with extensive shoals covering around half of the surface area. Some of the shoals even have names: Bird Island and Vessel Reef. As with much of the rest of the archipelago, these shoals shift, migrate, dissipate and accrete on an ongoing basis. The Bird Island shoal was once a nesting island serving the same function as Marsh Island currently does: a colonial bird rookery. It was impacted severely by Hurricane Hugo, and Hayes and Michel reported that it was planed off by the storm. They suggest that its growing accretion might classify it as an embryonic barrier island. Only time will tell.

Though it appears that Bulls Bay and the Atlantic Ocean have little to differentiate them on the water, a line delineates the boundary—the Colregs Demarcation Line. It is marked by some large pilings that stretch across the bay. This line has tangible meaning for shrimpers, for it is illegal to trawl in the waters inshore of these pilings. The line of poles makes it clear whether a trawler is on the right side of the line.

The fact that shrimpers might want to work these waters at the risk of the significant consequences indicates that the shallow waters and muddy bottom are excellent conditions to support a shrimp nursery. The frenzy that occurs in the bay in the recreational shrimp baiting season in the fall puts this body of water on the map as the number one spot in the Lowcountry for this activity.

The shallow waters of Bulls Bay provide the nurturing conditions for other forms of marine life. One family of fish with important nurseries in these waters is the shark. Similar to loggerhead turtles returning to Cape Island for reproduction and the laying of eggs, a number of shark species return to Bulls Bay to either release their young (viviparous) or lay eggs (oviparous). These nurseries, occupying only a very small portion of the species range, are the locations where the females go to lay eggs or deposit their young and where, naturally, the gravid females, neonates and young juveniles are found. Larger sharks do not stay in the shallow waters—a bonus for the young sharks since their main predators are bigger sharks. Species of carcharhinoid sharks identified with the Bulls Bay nurseries are blacknose, spinner, finetooth, blacktip, sandbar, dusky, Atlantic sharpnose, scalloped hammerhead and smooth dogfish sharks.

While sharks and other fishes come here to begin their lives, many craft and ships have sailed here at the end of their careers, often prematurely. These disasters were often the consequences of natural forces, though human forces and error also played a role. One loss of a small craft occurred on March 18, 1843. Captain Sherwood of the brig *Emily* reported sighting twenty miles to the southeast of Cape Romain a boat with four Negroes. These castaways reported that their sloop, owned by Mr. Manigault and carrying a load of wood, had sunk in Bulls Bay. They tried to reach shore in their boat, but the strong winds pushed them out to sea. They had been in the boat for twenty-four hours when rescued by the crew of the *Emily*. In an earlier time, another black boater aboard a canoe was found over forty miles off the cape by a Captain Lawrence in a vessel bound for Charleston from New York in June 1788. He reported that the man was traveling on a voyage to Guinea and was without provisions or water. What mental state would have triggered this voyage: desperation, resignation or suicidal depression?

Man-made forces certainly played a large role in ship losses—in navigation errors, but even more acutely in armed conflict during the Civil War. The need for the Confederacy to keep the engines of war running required money. Getting goods to available markets was critical, and the rice of the Santee River plantations was transported to Charleston. The Federal blockade did not allow the schooners to make the passage outside of the barrier islands, so the inland passage was used, with the bay crossing being challenging and exposed to the sea.

One of the blockaders taking up station off of Bulls Bay in 1862 was the USS *Restless*, commanded by Lieutenant Edward Conroy. He soon observed three to four vessels a day cruising across the shallow waters of the bay and out of reach of his ship. Intelligence was gathered from two escaped slaves off of the schooner *Theodore Stoney*, one of the vessels plying the inland passage. Conroy learned that twenty-five schooners and sloops were involved in this commerce. His crew, investigating the wreck of a sloop on a bay shoal, found that the *Theodore Stoney* and three other vessels were at anchor in the northwestern corner of the bay. With several ships' boats, Conroy's men attacked and took these craft, which were carrying a total of seventy-five hundred bushels of rice. Since there was no wind to sail off, and with Confederate forces nearby, the four vessels were burned and sunk in the bay.

Bulls Bay

During this same period, two larger vessels were also taken in Bulls Bay. Conroy and the *Restless* chased the blockade runner *Scotia*, commanded by the soon-to-be-famous Henry Sterling Lebby. She was cut off by the *Restless*, whose armed boats captured the *Scotia*, though Lebby and her crew escaped. In 1864, another blockade runner, the *Julia*, was on her second trip into Charleston when a storm forced her into Bulls Bay. Having run aground, boats from the blockader *Acadia* captured her.

Early in the twentieth century, a poignant human drama occurred in the bay. The drama centered on R.H. (Hepburn) Morrison, a resident of McClellanville and grandfather of Gene Morrison. Many of Hepburn Morrison's work endeavors revolved around the water. Gene recalled that his grandfather was small but hard as steel and known as the "bully" of the village. At the Cape Island parties, Hepburn would accept challenges in bouts of wrestling, particularly with men visiting from other towns. According to Gene, his grandfather bested all comers. Once Gene went clamming with his grandfather near Lighthouse Island, and the elder Morrison told him about his prowess. To demonstrate, Hepburn took his adolescent grandson out on the beach and threw some moves on him, hurling and pinning him to the sand.

One component of R.H. Morrison's maritime enterprises was the commerce in moving freight and passengers between McClellanville and Charleston in his vessel, the *Spray*. In early fall 1900, a Captain Pepper had taken the *Spray* to Charleston and was on the return voyage with goods and ten passengers, including women and children. During this trip, a heavy coastal storm had been lashing the area with high winds and three days of rain. Upon return to the village, a fishing vessel reported that the *Spray* was waiting out the storm on the other side of the bay, most likely in the protected Bull Creek anchorage. Mr. Morrison was so concerned about the safety of people and goods that he embarked at daybreak to cross the bay in a round-bottomed sailing craft with a yawl rig, accompanied by a black crewman named Phillip Williams.

Despite his skills as a waterman, Hepburn capsized in the strong winds. With no way to right the vessel, the two men hung on to the upside-down boat. The large waves from the storm repeatedly broke and washed across them. Gene recounted that his grandfather told him that he and Williams reached across the hull to each other and locked their hands in a lifesaving grasp. He expressed to Gene that this human bond saved his life. Williams, despite growing up and working in the creek, was a non-swimmer, and he screamed in terror as the waves struck. The long exposure, outgoing tide and swallowing of salt water weakened him to the point that Hepburn had to hold him up. Williams died in his companion's arms. The tide took the capsized vessel with the men out Bulls Inlet, and somewhere, later in the day, Hepburn, due to his weakened condition, let go of the deceased Williams to save his own life.

The turn of the tide brought the boat and Hepburn into the breakers off Bull Island, and letting loose from the boat he began the swim toward shore. With clothes gone, Hepburn made it to the beach, exhausted and naked. Crawling above the high-tide line, he buried himself in the sand to reduce exposure. Awakened by the pouring rain on his face and strong chills, he set off along the beach in the dark, determined to find Phillip Williams. Williams's body was never found.

A ravaging thirst stimulated him to search out water. A nearby source was the cistern behind the Bull Island lighthouse. He called for help when near the building, and the keeper, Halvor Svendsen, came to his assistance, carrying him back to his quarters. Svendsen and his wife worked to warm Hepburn with clothes, blankets and warm beverages. Clearly still feverish the next morning, he walked around the point to attempt to catch the *Spray* preparing to cross the bay. He was fortunate to do so and learned that another vessel had seen from the anchorage the capsized yawl being washed out to sea. The word had already reached the village that Hepburn was lost, and when coming in to Jeremy Creek in the *Spray*, he took the helm to reassure concerned family and friends waiting at the dock. For a few days after this event, still recovering from his illness, Hepburn yelled out to Williams from his fever: "Hold on!"

Bulls Bay is a body of water avoided by most boaters, and many cruisers in the ICW are barely aware of its existence. Boaters mainly skirt its ends from Anderson Creek and Five Fathom Creek, though they invade it for the fall shrimp baiting season. Much is to be learned by marine biologists of its marine life and nurseries. For those who know these waters, it is often a place of beauty. As the poet Robert Woodward Barnwell penned in his description of the bay as a Bowl of Beauty: "'Old silver bowl' was flashing sapphire lights and flame."

June 22, 2006

Low tide Jack's Creek, 11:42 a.m.; Jeremy Creek, 12:09 p.m. Predicted winds S 5–10 knots, then SE 10–15 knots.

The wind is flat at the Romain Retreat landing at 10:00 a.m. My initial thought is to head out Venning Creek, but with the low tide approaching, I instead head out Anderson Creek. I rig and push out, noticing the flag to the south hanging limp; perhaps there is a little north breeze. A couple of puffs come toward me in the ICW, and the southwest direction pushes us across the ICW toward the creek entrance. It is too good to be true, and as it fades, I grab my paddle and assist the forward movement with the remaining outgoing tide. I hit the oyster bottom and notice all around the large intertidal area exposed. I paddle through the next long straight and see a fisherman ahead in the next bend. The breeze is filling in, but unfortunately it is in the nose, defying the marine forecast. So we beat to windward and give the creek banks some space to avoid running aground.

The sky is overcast, and the darkness of some clouds suggests potential showers. We make it around several bends, heading toward the Shark Hole. Occasionally we get a shift and hope it is going to the southeast or south, but obstinately the direction keeps veering back to east. We pass another fisherman; the bay is in view, and the course is still to windward. We make it out the creek mouth into Bulls Bay but must still beat to stay in the deep water of the channel heading out to Bull Island's Northeast Point. This leg of the voyage is taking much longer than anticipated. The high dorsal fin of a dolphin appears ahead. We pass a couple of crab-trap buoys but a third turns out to be a loggerhead, ducking into a dive followed by its hind flippers. We continue the beat out, noticing the size of Bird Island shoal to the north.

On the inlet side of the Northeast Point there are people barely discernable on the beach. The light wind has me contemplating the planned voyage: my first crossing of Bulls Bay from Anderson Creek to Five Fathom Creek and landing at Jeremy Creek. I am recovering from an injury, and staying on the starboard tack for the majority of this trip will be necessary. Several events around Cape Island contributed to this upper-back pain. In April, while assisting in the building of the loggerhead hatcheries on Cape Island,

I perhaps was overzealous with the use of posthole diggers and noticed afterward some upper-back discomfort. Soon forgetting this strain, in May, after a long sail out to the North Point of Cape Island, I faced a long beat against a strong southwest wind up Cape Romain Harbor before entering the shelter of Horsehead Creek. The hour of holding the mainsheet by hand, mostly with the left hand, flared the back discomfort into pain that kept me awake for a number of nights and eventually led me to seek help from physical therapy. For several weeks I have wanted to get out on the water but have avoided sailing until today. Though I'm ready to heal, I hope the long starboard tack will keep the sheet out of my left hand and the stress off of my injured upper back.

Farther on, toward the Northeast Point, there is another island ahead, and I'm not sure what it is. Deciding to take a closer look at this isle, I steer for a landing, hitting the daggerboard several times, but finally make landfall. I step out on this sand isle for the first time and, walking around, find on several high spots some cannonball jellyfish and two self-buried horseshoe crabs. The isle at low tide has a sizable area of sand, most likely completely covered at the highest tides. (Two years later, I found this isle to be accreting, with a much higher elevation than Bird Island shoal. Dozens of pelicans, and even more black skimmers, were arrayed across this sandy isle.)

This transient isle is typical of many along this dynamic coast. One of these sand "bumps" grew outside of Key Inlet, located about ten miles north between Raccoon Key and Lighthouse Island. When surveyed in 1956, its area was thirty acres. This sandy isle with dunes was outside of the wildlife refuge, and a McClellanville resident made a claim on it. A fourteen-foot structure with screen windows and prop-out shutters was built, and the island retreat was aptly named Cool Breeze. It was enjoyed for a few years before the isle receded and finally disappeared. I imagine its sands now make up some of the current barrier islands and shoals around Key Inlet.

Upon returning to *Kingfisher* I notice several pelicans flying by and heading north across the bay, and they point the way for our course. Another sand isle stretches toward the northeast and then shoals with small waves. Smooth water appears inside of the shoals, separating the bay from the ocean, and my lunch and open water bottle sit steadily on deck. Marsh Island is visible and closer than anticipated. Markers lead the way into Five Fathom Creek far off to the east; our course is midway between these two landmarks. *Kingfisher* encounters small swells now, with a little break here and there and an occasional touch of the daggerboard on the bottom. Pelicans, royal terns and laughing gulls head across the bay and out to sea. Astern, another loggerhead stares and then dives. We are picking our way through areas of small waves abeam of Marsh Island and begin to head toward range markers. We could head in toward Sett Creek but opt for Five Fathom Creek. The White Banks glow white off to leeward.

I bring *Kingfisher* up to a close reach and can see the lighthouses out by the cape in the distance. Another loggerhead rises fifty yards astern. A large flight of birds head to the east, and they pass the range marker close to the water. These two-dozen pelicans bear a course to Marsh Island. We easily follow the markers in toward Sandy Point. A small trawler is heading out of the creek into the bay, bearing southeast into the wind. We are closehauled now in the course toward the Sandy Point isle. Mud sediments darken the southwest point, with mounds of shells beyond. It is about two hours past low water, and there is a strong flood past the markers.

I make a quick stop on this isle for a dip and look at the shell accumulation—deep piles of mostly oysters. We are once again sailing, and another small trawler appears heading into Five Fathom Creek. Soon we are reaching in this creek and enjoying the strong, favorable flood. A cloud of birds follows the trawler, and ahead another loggerhead surfaces to breathe. The trawler slows and turns to haul in its nets. We pass and see that she is the *Miss Agatha*, hailing from Cedar Island. A crowd of pelicans float in the water behind her stern. I ease off and run into the creek's long stretch to the northwest, noting that the *Miss Agatha* has finished hauling her nets and is coming on. Our course is now to the northeast, requiring heading up and sheeting in. In Town Creek, a sail of a multihull is moving north across the marsh. Coming out into the ICW with a strong current, I see two more sailboats with sails up motoring north. The wind is fading some, but it is no problem making it into Jeremy Creek. It is relatively quiet as we glide in: as relaxing and peaceful a landing as the bay crossing has been.

THE INLAND PASSAGE

Getting to know one's way around the Cape Romain area takes some time and study. One must learn the numerous waterways and creeks, along with their depth of water at various tides. The channels across the shallow bays and the sounds must also become familiar. When various landmarks on the islands and in the marsh become part of one's memory, then passages through the archipelago open up these worlds to the boater.

I was initially led to the historical passage through the archipelago—the inland passage—by several hints. The names of several creeks gave me pause: Congaree Boat Creek, Santee Path Creek and Santee Pass. I was to learn that these creeks were part of a historical passage from Charleston to the Santee River. This chain of creeks and channels was used not by oceangoing vessels but by shallow-draft craft: canoes and smaller sloops and schooners. The passage was the ultimate local knowledge, passed on from mariner to mariner via experience and word of mouth. I learned, in depth, about this inland passage through the essay "Names and Places" in the appropriately named *Inland Passages* by William Baldwin.

The following is Baldwin's description of the route of the inland passage from the Santee River:

> *A traveler of this inland passage would have left Alligator Creek at Ramhorn Creek, then passed through the narrow Needles Eye and into Mill*

Tracing the Cape Romain Archipelago

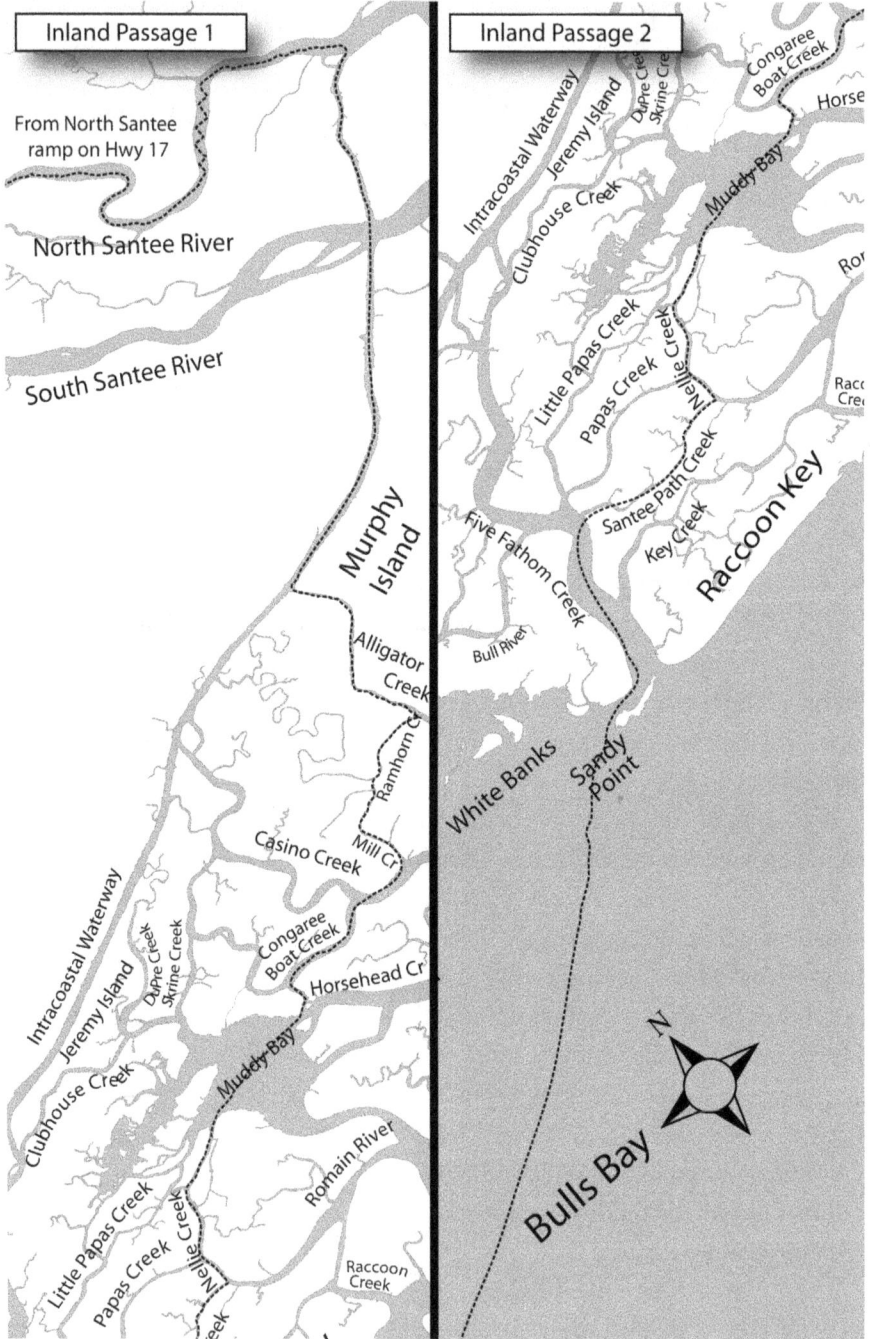

Creek, which carried him into Casino Creek…Turning right, our boatman

The Inland Passage

would enter Congaree Boat Creek….Next he would approach Horsehead Island, which was probably marked by a horse head–shaped bush or an actual animal's skull. The creek beside it is Cowhead. From there he crossed Muddy Bay, formerly Oyster Bay, and entered Papas Creek, which is the Gullah or Geechee pronunciation of porpoise, and like Cassena had fallen victim to army engineers' transcribing. A turn down thirty-foot-deep Five Fathoms Creek would carry him past White Banks, Vessel Reef and Bird Bank, out through Bull Channel, Bull Narrows and on to Charles Town, which was also Charleston.

It appears that the knowledge of this passage is ancient. When John Lawson began his great journey through the Carolinas at the end of 1700, he began at Charles Towne. He traveled in a large dugout canoe holding ten people and was led by a Native American guide, who was accompanied by his wife and two other Native Americans. In the journey from town to the Santee River, they encountered some of the difficulties of this inland passage. Despite it being winter, when they stopped for the night, they met with large clouds of mosquitoes and flies. But one of the biggest problems of the passage was the crossing of Bulls Bay. When Lawson and his party attempted their crossing, they encountered a northwest gale that combined with the strong tide to create rough waters, "which put us in some Danger of being cast away." They returned to Bull Island for another night and, when heading north toward the South Santee again, "went thro' the Creeks, which lie between the Bay and the main Land."

With the importance of the Santee River plantations in the eighteenth century, the travel between town and country made this inland passage a vital means of commerce. Harriet Horry of Hampton Plantation used a small schooner to transport goods through the inland passage. One of the most important merchants and plantation owners of this century was Henry Laurens. At one time he owned five plantations as part of a large and extremely lucrative empire, an enterprise coordinated from his Charles Towne home in Ansonborough. One of his plantations, Wambaw, was just off the South Santee River on Wambaw Creek. Part of the engine of his empire was slave labor, and one set of specialized skills of blacks was as boatmen, whether in canoes or schooners. African Americans were regular voyagers on this inland passage, as we can gather from Laurens's correspondence. A main vessel between town and country was the *Wambaw*, a small (fifteen ton) schooner carrying "five Negroes." Besides the transport of barrels of rice and shingles from the plantation, Laurens also would request hogs, turkeys, geese and ducks for his table. Laurens, in his voluminous correspondence, would send specific instructions to the captain of the *Wambaw*. In September 1765, he received word from the master of the *Wambaw* through the slave Achilles that the vessel had gone aground. Laurens sent the following message:

> He [Achilles] *did not get down till Saturday Night very late & said he had waded thro so much water that your Letter was quite dissolved, but from the Account that he gave me I immediately (the next morning) order'd an Anchor, Cable, Twine, pilot, & four other hands in my large Canoe to be sent to you. The People went away early on Monday Morning & got to the place where you had been aground, that very day, but hearing that you have proceeded to George Town they returned.*

In that the refloated *Wambaw* had proceeded to Georgetown, the canoe would have traveled from Charles Towne through the inland passage to the place of grounding. The fact that Laurens sent along a "pilot" indicated that not everyone knew how to navigate this complex course.

The black boatmen would have freedom traveling the inland passage from plantation to town, having to stop for the night at various landings along the passage. In his correspondence, Laurens often complained about his black boatmen and his suspicions that they were robbing him, indicating to one overseer, "Pray be so good as to give a watchful eye to the behavior of Abraham and his gang." Laurens alerted the overseer at Wambaw to another boatman, Amos, as having "a great inclination to turn Rum Merchant," suspecting he was sending rum by Laurens's flatboat to Mayrant's Landing, and charged the overseer with prosecuting a caught Amos with "39 sound Stripes."

Over fifty years later, Denmark Vesey, a free black man from Charleston, probably traveled up the inland passage to gather support for the planned Charleston insurrection from the "French Negroes along the Santee River." Perhaps some of those slaves along the Santee River who heard Vesey prior to the planned date arrived in the group of fifty

The Inland Passage

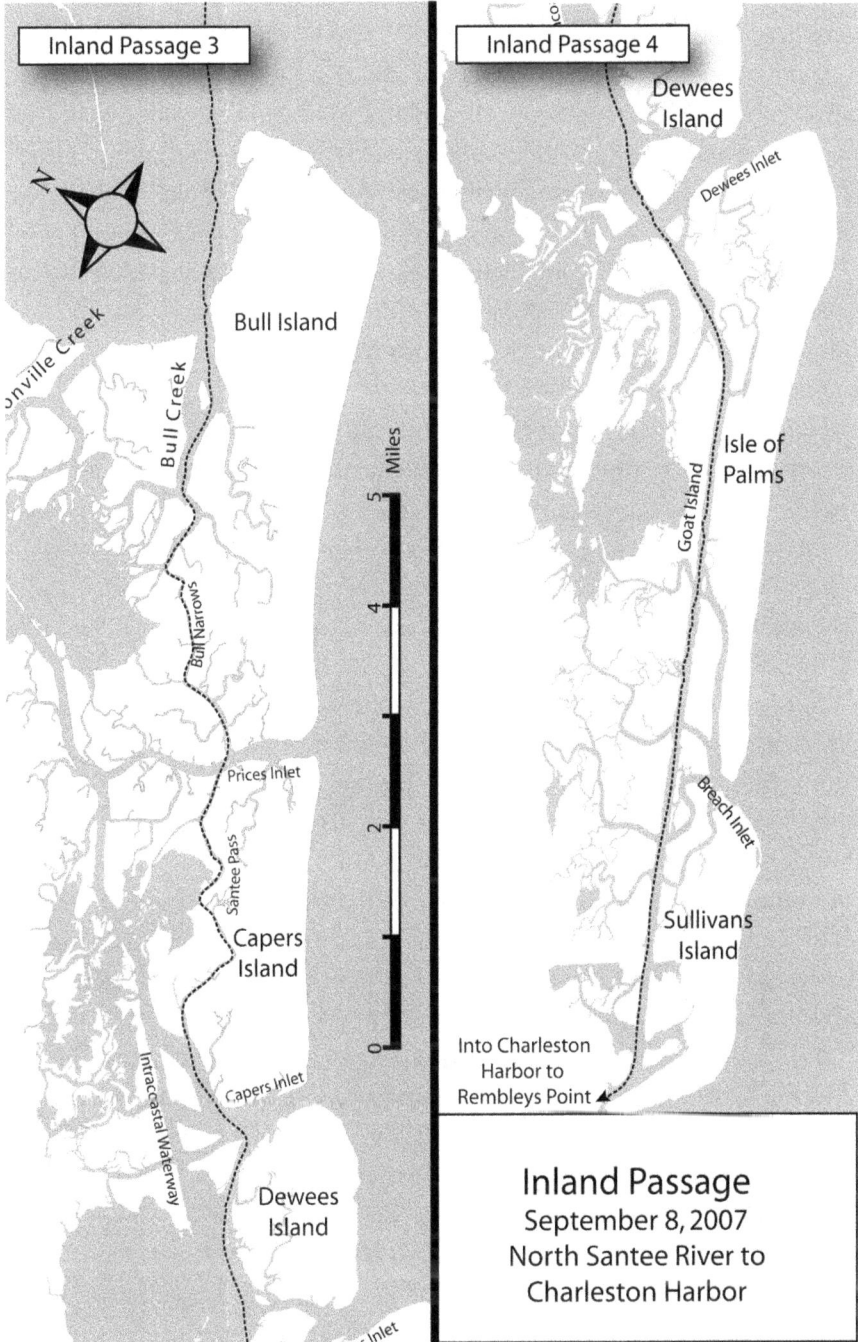

Inland Passage 3

Inland Passage 4

Dewees Island

Dewees Inlet

Bull Island

Onville Creek

Bull Creek

Isle of Palms

Goat Island

Bull Narrows

5 Miles

4

Prices Inlet

Breach Inlet

Santee Pass

2

Capers Island

Sullivans Island

Intracoastal Waterway

Into Charleston Harbor to Rembleys Point

Capers Inlet

Dewees Island

s Inlet

Inland Passage
September 8, 2007
North Santee River to Charleston Harbor

slaves on that fateful day of June 17, 1822, after making the inland passage. Vesey's revolt failed, and he and a number of his confederates were hanged in Charleston.

Another successful revolt preceded Vesey's failed one—the War of Independence—and similarly, the inland passage was utilized as an important conduit of information. Francis Marion employed several covert allies in sending and receiving intelligence. A Captain Bellamy used trading missions in a periauger through the inland passage between Charleston and Georgetown as a cover for intelligence missions. A boy, George Spidle, would step off at various landings along the way and take advertising handbills to the plantations. He would leave letters for Marion in hollow trees shown to him near the landings.

The difficulty of navigating this inland passage had been a concern for some time. With the advent of steam use for propulsion, a protected passage along the east coast became an important work under consideration by the federal government. In December 1813, a document was prepared by Robert Fulton, titled "Report on the Practicability of Navigating with Steam Boats, on the Southern Waters of the United Sates, from the Chesapeake to the River St. Mary's." Fulton used the surveys of John D. Delacy to review the existing waterways and their potential for the creation of a protected waterway. Fulton offered descriptive comments on the various creeks and sounds, from "This is a fine sheet of water" to "Here the meanders of the channel are great, and some of the angles it forms so very acute, that it will require cutting." He noted in places that there were stakes marking a channel. For another section, he commented, "The intersection of the creeks are so numerous, that a good pilot is not only indispensable, but the true channel should be marked."

During the Civil War, the inland passage was for a while a protected waterborne route for the movement of goods and people between Charleston and the Santee River. After watching schooners and sloops making runs through this passage, Lieutenant Edward Conroy of the USS *Restless* starting sending armed boats after these vessels. After a spectacular first night success with capturing, sinking and burning four vessels in the bay, Conroy's men followed this up a week later with entering into the natural waterways of the inland passage and capturing four more vessels in two days: the schooner *George Washington*, the schooner *Julia Worden*, a schooner belong to a Mr. Thompson and Mr. Doar's sloop, *Mary Louisa*.

In 1902, a project by the federal government enlarged the channel from Charleston to McClellanville. The inland passage had places where the water depth was not more than one foot at low tide. More troublesome were the open sections of the passage across Bulls Bay, where vessels were exposed to the open sea. The 1902 project deepened the waterway to four feet deep, sixty feet wide and moved the channel completely from the open area of the Bulls Bay crossing. In 1935, the Army Corps of Engineers received funding to deepen and widen the waterway (ten feet and ninety feet, respectively). This work was completed in June 1935. Five years later, the channel depth was increased to twelve feet. The inland passage ended as a passage of choice for commercial and recreational boaters alike. Its memory will mainly live through the names of creeks.

SEPTEMBER 8, 2007

Low tide 12:36 p.m. Bulls Bay. Predicted winds NE 15–20 knots.
Tropical Storm Watch.

Before 5:00 a.m., from the perspective of my deck, there is an unusual clarity of the night sky, with Orion leading the constellation display. A meteor streaks across the sky. In the distance, the sound of surf on Bull Island rumbles. A trace of the imminent northeast wind perhaps rustles an oak's leaves. An early start is in order for this long-awaited, and recently obsessed about, voyage. The plan is to head out the Santee River and recreate the southern trip to Charleston Harbor via the pre–Intracoastal Waterway course: the inland passage. The high pressure and northeast flow have been dominant this week, and today marks what should be an ideal tide day, with low tide a little after noon. Theoretically, the outgoing tide will help me out of the river and continue out through the creeks of the Cape Romain marshes into Bulls Bay. If all goes well and progress is optimal, the incoming tide will bring us into Charleston Harbor for a takeout at Remley's Point, a landing on the Wando River a little past the Cooper River Bridge. This will be a very ambitious passage in *Kingfisher*, made all the more challenging by having no option for starting in the

Santee River except for the public landing at the North Santee Bridge over Highway 17.

My wife, Susan, and I trail *Kingfisher*, starting about 5:45 a.m., heading north up Highway 17. We leave Charleston County as we cross over the South Santee Bridge, and traveling over the Santee Delta in the predawn light, we climb over the North Santee Bridge. Just past the bridge we turn off about 180 degrees to the public landing. It is completely empty but noisy, with the electrical substation right there. It is before 6:30 a.m., as planned, and soon *Kingfisher* is launched and rigged. We say our goodbyes, and Susan takes the trailer home as I push off in the cool morning. With the temperature below 70 and the water above 80, water vapor is smoking off of the river's surface.

As the day dawns, the partial moon and Venus are still prominent. A little breeze is coming from behind and is tangible in the water vapor blowing along, in places swirling in gyres. Civilization is not quickly left behind, since the eighteen-wheel vehicles going over the North Santee Bridge grid decking send the staccato drumming blaring for miles. Slowly, river sound becomes more prominent, and the first kingfisher of the day heralds dawn on the north bank. A little farther, a pileated woodpecker joins the sound makers, along with the splash of a good-sized fish off to port. A much louder splash close by along the south bank is an alligator, perhaps wondering who invades his realm.

The wind is spotty, and since the landing is about an hour behind the coastal tide readings, there is some adverse flow. I use the paddle liberally, recognizing the far northern start for the planned trip. Through the first large bend in the river, the high-pitched revolutions of an outboard starting up come from behind at the landing. Soon, two men in a small, narrow skiff race by, dressed fully for the early morning chill. This craft is the first in a steady parade of boats launching at the landing and heading downriver for fishing beyond. After several more bends in the river, the progress is improving with the wind. I wonder how far upriver the blue crabs come, and I look for that first crab pot. The float appears ahead on a long, straight reach, and a tern flying by is another indicator of the approaching coast. I roughly measure distance and time and, though we're making good progress, wish we were farther along. I continue with these thoughts, letting go of time milestones and appreciating where I am right now—clearly an amazing new world on this river.

The Inland Passage

Sunrise on the North Santee River at the beginning of the inland passage.

One difference with these waters and others I travel seems to be the increased numbers of African Americans out on the water. Both the North and South Santee communities, predominately black, are not far from the public landing by the bridge. I'm sure the boaters heading by have not seen many sailing craft on this section of the river, and definitely not this early, but each boater passes with the comforting friendly wave of boaters everywhere. I do not see any of the passing boats on my passage to the ICW, so clearly the fishing grounds are farther along, perhaps toward the mouth of the river.

After a sharp S-bend in the river, I pass the entrance to Six Mile Creek, one of the original creeks cutting through to the South Santee River. It is a very convoluted passage, appearing three to four times the actual distance to the other river. I will head on to the ICW and the Fourmile Creek Canal. My inland passage course today is not historically pure, since I take advantage of modern conveniences: being dropped off at the landing this morning, following the marine forecast for days via the NOAA website and utilizing the dug channels of the ICW here and there. And I embark on the trusty *Kingfisher*, built of modern materials, though I'm sure my friends and fellow boaters would hotly dispute my viewing the use of a Sunfish for this passage as a modern convenience. My plan is to follow the pre–Intracoastal Waterway course as much as possible and avoid the ICW.

The advantage of modern weather forecasting is significant, and experienced boaters have this information readily available. The marine forecast is for northeast winds, fifteen to twenty knots, perhaps the ideal winds for this trip. Yet overnight, a low sitting off the coast all week finally organized into subtropical storm Gabrielle, and a tropical storm watch is posted for the North and South Carolina coasts. There is no danger today, and winds are not predicted to pick up until late tonight. While the chance of thunderstorms seems to be included in every summer forecast, there is none today. Hurricane forecasting is helping to save lives every hurricane season, giving coastal residents the warning needed to be safe. My family and I heeded the warnings and evacuated before Hurricane Hugo, one of the better decisions I have made in my life. The unfortunate residents of the low islands I will soon be passing, Cedar and Murphy, had no such warning in 1822, when that year's great storm drowned many of the people on those plantations.

Coming around a bend, a long northeast reach of the river awaits, requiring the associated windward work. I look for the entrance on the south bank of a possible canal cutting across to the South Santee. I had already decided that unless I had local knowledge of such a small waterway being navigable I would not attempt a shortcut, and the entrance is not at all inviting for such an adventure. So we beat to windward, and with the wind solid, perhaps at seven to eight knots, the windward sailing is excellent, with the sky a clear blue and the waterway only occupied by *Kingfisher*. The river is wide, there is plenty of depth and the tide has clearly turned in my favor. Progress on one port tack across the river is not very good, and on the tack back to starboard I raise the daggerboard all the way up. I find that *Kingfisher* was hampered by the dragging of floating reeds, which now pass astern in our wake. Shortly afterward, I am able to bear off for the last section before the canal across to the South Santee, passing Minim Island on the north side of the river. The opening to Atkinson Creek appears in the south bank, and I know this is a passage to the south river from Nathaniel Bishop's journey south in his paper canoe. The marker for the ICW is ahead, and shortly I bear off and begin the run south.

Initially, the tide is opposed to our course, but the wind is solid so progress is good. The marsh on the left bank is the western part of Cedar Island. I estimate that I will reach the South Santee River about 9:30 a.m. A barrier on the inland passage is the water depth of Muddy Bay, and getting there in time for the crossing is of some concern. However, I am mentally prepared to take whatever comes and what the conditions will allow me to do.

Running with the wind, I am pleased with the rig and performance of *Kingfisher*. Running down the beach of Bull Island last month in a strong breeze, I was concerned by a steering problem with the wind directly behind. The connection between the upper and lower booms had also come apart that day, requiring a hasty jury rig. Taking the advice of Randall Swan, harbor pilot and small boat racer extraordinaire, I had cut back the corroded aluminum end and re-bored and fastened the connecting eyebolts. It has been tested on several sails, with running and jibing the key tests. There will be plenty of this action today, but so far so good. Additionally, an adjustment made since the last sail eliminated the slop between the rudder and tiller connection existing since the rudder replacement in 2004. And one other adjustment is consciously being made by the helmsman: heeling the boat to windward when running downwind. After years of Laser sailing, this hull trim to windward seems self-destructive as a prelude to a death roll and windward capsize, but in the Sunfish the hard chine makes a difference in stability. I am noticing an improved helm in the puffs already with this hull trim. One other detail I attend to on this leg of the sail is tying down all of the loose gear in the boat as a preparation for the Bulls Bay crossing.

The sailing conditions continue to improve to ideal. I recall an old black carpenter I once worked with in Wilmington, North Carolina. When fitting together a joint between two pieces of trim, if the fit was very good he would say, "If I had it any better than this I wouldn't want to have it!" This seems an appropriate sentiment for today's weather, pushing *Kingfisher* along on our serpentine course to the southwest.

A channel marker appears ahead, signaling the confluence with the South Santee River. We run out into this waterway and are grabbed by the outgoing tide. We jibe over to cut across this watercourse, and with the breeze now at ten to twelve knots, we easily make it into the continuation of the ICW. During our circumnavigation of Murphy Island in June, we came along this course for the first time. I recall that initially the outgoing tide was opposed but soon found it pushing us along. That is also the case today as we run down the waterway along Murphy Island. Originally, this waterway was Alligator Creek, which has been widened, straightened and deepened; the sign of dredge spoil is on the banks. Only one boat has passed us since leaving the North Santee River. As we approach the turnoff of Alligator Creek to the southeast, branching off of the ICW but originally the only waterway through here, the sound of a boat trails from astern, and the craft appears as we jibe into this course.

Alligator Creek marks the southwest side of Murphy Island and flows out to Cape Romain Harbor. We are reaching across this northeast wind, though with the tide dropping there is some wind shadow from the bank and the parallel dike. The boat astern turns into the creek behind us and is motoring slowly along. As it approaches, I see it is a pontoon boat, and we move over to the west bank as it heads by. I am following the chart carefully now, looking for the entrance to Ramhorn Creek. One creek mouth appears, though it does not correspond to the bends in the chart. A little farther along, the mouth of this creek opens and invites our jibe to the west. Bishop and his paper canoe missed this turn, and he passed out through Alligator Creek into the open water beyond.

We sailed through here earlier this year in the opposite direction on the way out to Murphy. The tide is opposed to our direction, but the breeze behind pushes us along. While identical to many other waterways through the Lowcountry salt marsh, a distinction of Ramhorn Creek is the connection to Mill Creek through the narrow Eye of the Needle. I look ahead for this junction, and when the creek bends to starboard, the small opening beckons our entrance. Jibing in, the sail, boomed out to starboard, brushes through the marsh grass. I wonder later if this waterway could have been dug to make this connection, since it is about fifty yards long and dead straight. Swishing through the *Spartina*, we soon come out into our next waterway, Mill Creek. Bishop had described the Eye of the Needle as an old steamboat passage, but if that is the case, this waterway has clearly filled in from his time.

The passage to the next large waterway, Casino Creek, is uneventful until the last section. A crabber rapidly motors past the outside of the creek mouth and behind an oyster bank. I don't know what creek he has charged into but find out when we get out into this larger waterway. He has cut in between the oyster bank and the marsh bank to pick up one of his crab pots, and he has not only run aground but has also wrapped the pot buoy line around his engine's propeller. He disentangles the line from the prop as I hail him in passing. With more room to sail, we pick up speed, a good compensation for bucking an outgoing tide. We are planing and soon bear off at the fork where Casino Creek heads up to the north, taking the Congaree Boat Creek turn to the southwest. There is some cloud cover along here. The dropping water has us low in the creek, and I am not able to see the observation tower from this perspective. With the turn to the south in the narrow waterway connecting us with Muddy Bay, we pick up the push of the outgoing tide again.

So here we are at Muddy Bay at the moment of truth. It is 11:15 a.m., giving us about one hour and twenty minutes until low water. The northeast wind will help with water depth—will it be enough? We strike out across the bay, taking a westerly course. There are no landmarks for the entrance across the bay into Nellie Creek, so I take the opposite direction to the easterly course made last year on my first trip across this shallow body of water, navigating with the compass. There is not another boat in sight, and the visibility is excellent. The green marsh of the far side of the bay appears. I am prepared for the worst: running aground and getting stuck through the low tide and beyond, and I will accept that outcome. Halfway across, my bearing a little south of west appears good, as has been the progress on this run. The wind has been strengthening, and we are close to planing. Gradually, the progress becomes a little sluggish, *Kingfisher*'s wake begins to kick up and it appears we are dragging the bottom. Pulling up the daggerboard, I work to make it through, perhaps only a hundred yards to go. Sensing rudder drag as well, I move forward and trim the hull more to windward, effectively reducing the rudder's depth. Different color water appears ahead—deeper. We make it through and now have the water depth for the easy entrance into Nellie Creek. It has been a fine crossing, made with little time to spare.

The dual factors of the wind from behind and the last hour of the outgoing tide are speeding us along with plenty of sailing room. We pass a first creek mouth to starboard, and this must be Little Papas Creek. The familiar oyster bar in the shape of a giant alligator is off to port farther on. Minutes pass before the entrance to what I think is Papas Creek, though I wonder if this is instead my turn for the Santee Path Creek. I recall that the opening should just be a little farther, and it will not be a long backtrack if we have passed it. But the chart is right; with the bend to the east of Nellie Creek, the Santee Path Creek opens into the marsh to the west, and we jibe and enter this familiar waterway.

We easily pass the little section of opposed outgoing tide before we catch the main flow heading to Five Fathom Creek, our next main waterway to join. An outboard zooms by—the first boat seen since the crabber in Casino Creek. The creek name, Santee Path, is another reminder of the passage made by watermen for years passing between the Santee River and Charleston. The same name will be picked up again behind Capers Island. As we leave the narrow creek for the openness of Five Fathom Creek, I connect on a cellphone with my daughter, Sara, at that moment at the Isle of Palms beach. Before hanging up, I ask about the size of the surf. She tells me it is not big and mainly breaking on the shore. This is good news, since the marine forecast for seas of four to five feet offshore had me concerned about the Bulls Bay crossing. It seems like everything is lined up right for this trip. When Henry Laurens sent his relentless correspondence to his plantation manager at Wambaw, he several times instructed the communication to be passed on to his schooner captain to "not lose the wind"—meaning to take advantage of a favorable wind direction and flow. This wind would have been optimal for the several days needed to make that trip from the Wambaw Plantation to his Ansonborough wharf.

We are really moving south in Five Fathom now, at times on a full plane, and are among a few other boaters ahead and astern. I use the mainsail cleats on deck without thought for securing the sail and steer with my leg or foot, leaving my hands free for other tasks. Prior to the bay, I pull out a snack and water, replenishing carbs and fluids for the crossing. There are a couple of boats on the sandy end of Raccoon Key as the bay comes into view. The sight is encouraging; there are small waves on the first set of shoals, but behind them the waters look relatively calm. The wind is a solid fifteen to eighteen knots from the northeast, and I don't hesitate to commit to the jibe, heading out the old channel behind the Sandy Point remnant. The bank to starboard is very exposed with the low tide, and we avoid an oyster bed in the run out. There are no boats behind here fishing today, and in passing the refracted surf by the end of the Sandy Point remnant, we enter the waters of Bulls Bay at 12:25 p.m.

We jibe to a port tack broad reach for our initial heading out into the bay. There is one boat to be seen in these waters, the familiar crabber with the homemade roof on his craft. He heads in, bouncing along across the waves in the distance as I head in the opposite direction with the swells, already broken by the outer shoal but still with body and movement. There are old channel markers giving a heading to parallel, and farther on other markers seem to indicate areas of shoals, exposed by waves breaking all around. In fact, some of these markers are for the Line, the separation of Bulls Bay and the ocean. But our way seems easy, and the wind is allowing *Kingfisher* to surf on waves occasionally. I maximize the opportunities: steering to catch waves, pumping the mainsail to jump the hull on to a plane and moving forward and aft along the port deck vigorously to maintain the proper trim. I take care to avoid submarining the bow, both to keep water out of the cockpit or, worse, creating a pitchpole (going over end for end). I donned my lifejacket long ago in the marshes before Muddy Bay and must utilize my downwind sailing skills on this exciting ride. This experience brings to mind an old sailing term that fits what I am doing now: *scudding*, sailing at full bore with following wind and waves. All is lined up for an ultimate flow experience in the early stage of this Bulls Bay crossing.

We pass the White Banks a good distance off to starboard and see ahead, off the forward starboard quarter, the green of Marsh Island. But the most joyous sight is the outline of Bull Island to the southwest. Our passage will be through the inlet and into Bull Creek behind the island. I sight a second craft on this crossing—a commercial fishing vessel outside of the bay. It is not a traditional shrimp trawler and appears to have a large boom at almost a vertical attitude. Our course is taken off Bull Island, and the heading is southwest. We are making the crossing at a rapid pace and soon appear halfway there. Raccoon Key and Cape

Island disappeared some time ago, and only the faint elevations of the lighthouses are discernable.

We are three quarters of the way across the bay, and there is no water in the cockpit! This run is not over, for extensive cresting of waves indicating shoals appear ahead. It would not be an enviable task to sail back across the bay against the wind and waves. There is one last marker a little below my course, with waves around it, and I continue with my current course, prepared to pick my way through the breaking swells. I am working harder in the waves, making rapid sail and hull trim changes. *Kingfisher* and I are one in these moments. We take off on a wave and accelerate quickly as a section of the wave breaks just off the aft starboard quarter. I soon realize that my course is off, and what I thought was the Northeast Point is actually the Boneyard, much farther to the east. So I bear off to run with the waves, and we find our way in. We are off on one wave, and suddenly the bow is going under. I quickly move aft and head up to shake the bow out of this plunge. It is up, but not before I have put inches of water in the cockpit. There are waves all around now, not big but requiring full attention and effort. I reach down to pull the cork plug from the self-bailer, and the end breaks off in my hand. It is sheared off at the cockpit level, and fingernails will not dislodge it. So it is sponge, sail and look over my shoulder for the next breaking wave. I get some water out and continue to pick waves to either head up over the shoulder or surf.

The inlet is close now, and I see a boat in the distance, either on the Northeast Point or anchored. But ahead I see trouble—my navigation is way off. Between me and the inlet are exposed shoals, the sand island where I landed on my bay crossing last year. So a quick decision is required: either jibe and head back, going through more waves to miss the shoals to the northeast, or see if I can squeeze by above these shoals on the inlet side. I choose the latter, heading up to a close reach and planing across the small waves along here. I start dragging my daggerboard and pulling it up higher than usual on a close reach. It is shallow, and there are small waves all along. The exposed shoal with standing birds is just to leeward. But I'm not turning back now and see a channel on the other side. I work to reduce my draft by staying on a plane, bouncing over the little waves. But I hit the board even when pulled up high, and now I brush the rudder. Using a little heel to leeward to reduce draft, we push

The Inland Passage

Black skimmers and royal terns, with other seabirds, taking flight in a stiff northeast wind on Bull Island's Northeast Point.

through this last little bit. Ready to bear off, the helm has no resistance, since my rudder has kicked up all the way. Moving aft, quickly pushing it down and bearing off before falling in irons, we are in the channel—smooth deep water between the shoal just passed and another flanking the east side of the inlet.

Birds line the shoals, with an abundance of black skimmers watching our passing and vocalizing their distinctive sounds. We have made the crossing, though the poor navigation created some exciting moments at the end. Standing up in the cockpit, I survey the scene: waves breaking for miles around, yet calm waters inside of the shoals to the west. Making mental notes on this learning experience, I check the time and realize that I made this Bulls Bay crossing in less than one hour. In celebration, I take off my hat and wave it high in the air at the two fishermen anchored off toward the island. Amazingly, now the incoming tide is pushing *Kingfisher* on our new course into Bull Creek for the next leg of the voyage. Being in my home waters is comforting, and the houses of Romain Retreat along the ICW clearly stick out in the distance. After the excitement in the bay, these waters seem placid as I pull out lunch and run in behind the island. It is also time to stand and stretch sore leg muscles, a routine repeated often today.

Several boats are anchored in Bull Creek fishing, and the waters and atmosphere are serene. The line of the channel is distinctive, with muddy waters to the east and clear blue channel waters adjacent. We pass an anchored boat on the edge, and the fisherman is releasing a ray, the predominant catch of the day. A pod of dolphins swims in the blue channel, heading northeast. We take the course to the east of the marsh island in the middle of the creek and then notice the USFWS dock down Summerhouse Creek before steering west to continue moving with the incoming waters of Bull Creek.

Earlier in this creek, I replaced my NOAA chart with a more detailed ICW chart to refer to the continued voyage toward the southwest, but in referring to it I realized that this chart does not have the entrance into Bull Narrows from Bull Creek. This is a very important detail, and though I have sailed through here several times, the reference is necessary. Nathaniel Bishop, in his paper canoe, had just received the local chart the day before from a U.S. survey vessel, but in making the passage he was overconfident and missed the correct branch. He ended up rowing a frustrating extra eight miles that day, backtracking to the correct course. I pull the NOAA chart back out of a water bag and re-place it in the chart holder for reference.

While I am making sure to find the correct branch into Bull Narrows, my casual approach to sailing has a consequence. I have been sailing along with the sheet cleated, steering at times with my foot or knee or sitting on the tiller extension to have both hands available for other tasks. I have even been making one-handed jibes. A casually made jibe in Bull Creek puts *Kingfisher* up on its beam ends. With a view of the daggerboard coming out of the water, the hull comes back down before it is necessary to jump on the board as a last ditch effort to terminate a full capsize. In hindsight, I did not trim the sheet in smartly when rounding, and the loose sheet flipped up over a sail clip and prevented the sail's release after the boom swung over. I don't recall this happening before, but I remind myself to sheet in on jibes at the correct time and not to get complacent about the remaining sail—there is a long way to go. In considering the remaining sail, it seems that Charleston Harbor is reachable before dark, and it is full speed to that end.

My attention to navigation pays off, since the entrance to Bull Narrows is not straightforward, and without chart reference, I would be guessing. But we are into the Narrows. Though we are sailing deep in the creek due to the low tide, the wind is from behind, and we continue to move along well. We are in the marsh world, and I don't really have a good view of the glorious island nearby. The navigation once in this waterway is quite straightforward, and no other craft are encountered until the last section before Price Inlet. A blue outboard sits anchored ahead, and its swing on the anchor line indicates the incoming tide from the approaching inlet. A couple lounge stretched out under the cover of their bimini top. They have found a very relaxing spot, away from the relatively busy waterway at the inlet. Once into Price's Creek, the view stretches out to the southeast to Little Bull's Island and the boats anchored along both Bull and Capers Islands. I recall landing on the south end of Bull a number of times in the past and remember that Bishop stopped here in his paper canoe to spend the night, staying with a Magwood in a house right by the inlet. This would have been a natural spot for voyagers along the inland passage to Santee or Charleston to stop.

We shoot quickly across the wide creek leading to the inlet and into the mouth of the next section of our course, the Santee Pass. Again, this waterway reflects in its name the passage to and from the Santee River. We are sailing along in a creek very similar to Bull Narrows but now behind Capers Island. The chart shows that farther ahead we will pass very close to the island. In passing a small creek penetrating into the marsh to port, a great blue heron picks up in flight, squawking loudly and continuously as he heads away. The serenity of the creek is soon disturbed by motor noise ahead; not just any engines but the buzzing of four personal watercraft rounding the bend and heading toward me. I move *Kingfisher* to the starboard side of the waterway to open up the channel. They are hot-dogging by, slaloming from creekside to creekside and jumping each other's wakes, but they respectfully form a line as they pass me. I speculate that they have rented these craft somewhere up the waterway and have found this passage. They have passed a boundary away from civilization, and it appears that in reverse I have also crossed this line.

We pass by a creek to starboard, giving a view out to Mark Bay, a small open area with exposed mud flats and oyster reefs. We soon bend sharply to the southwest, and the chart indicates that the creek runs almost right to the upland of Capers before bending to the northwest. At this bend, there is a substantial pier with a floating dock, part of the DNR presence in managing the island as a state property. The tide has been coming in for a little while now, and sitting up higher, the flowering of the marsh grass is more evident. We are now on a long straight to the west-northwest, and the wind is still showing no signs of moderation. Actually being able to complete the sail into Charleston Harbor appears a reality with the current position, time and conditions.

After a sharp bend to the southwest, the creek view ahead is of a more open body of water, Capers Creek. Once in this wide creek, the markers of the ICW appear to the west above the marsh, and the solitude of the passage we have enjoyed is coming to an end. This is reinforced when the harbingers of the end to peace, the personal watercraft quartet, zoom by, heading back to port. Numerous creeks—Capers, Whiteside, Toomer and Bullyard—join to form the wide waterway leading to Capers Inlet. Crossing the inner part of the inlet, the flotilla anchored off the end of Capers Island is assembled. The popularity of this landing spot is evident, and as we sail downwind of the flotilla the beat of loud rock music fills the air. Happily the breeze helps us to plane away, past this sonic disturbance of the environment.

The creek passing by the west side of Dewees Island opens up into a more open area, Bull Yard Sound, a large sheet of water with the ICW close by. Toward the mainland a bigger, shallow bay, Copahee Sound, is in view. There are many boats traveling up and down the ICW, and we stay away from the channel on the Dewees Island side, continuing to plane along at a good pace. The first sizable creek leading out to the southeast gives a view to the next inlet along the coast, Dewees Inlet. Before long, we are crossing the deep waters of Dewees Creek and have a better view of the inlet. Another weekend flotilla is enjoying the clear beautiful day here. Also in view is the northeastern end of Isle of Palms, with its high-rises in stark contrast to the undeveloped islands passed today.

The options for navigation are quite limited, and the course is alongside the ICW. The next section is called Seven Reaches, and we hug the eastern side. Very quickly, we come to the angled turn to the southwest and the narrow waterway between the Isle of Palms and Goat Island. I keep *Kingfisher* on the Goat Island side, running just outside of the dense array of docks. There is no effect from boat wakes since NO WAKE is clearly marked all along. The Isle of Palms side has a high density of docks, and the houses, apartments, condominiums and other developments are much denser than on Goat Island. The development around the Isle of Palms marina is particularly high, and a dock complex along the ICW is most likely the personal watercraft home for the riders seen earlier. The window in *Kingfisher*'s sail is not just an asset but also a safety factor to keep from running into docks. We are so close that occasionally I converse with people on the docks, and one party humorously compliments me for keeping my wake down.

I am working on refolding my chart in order to view Charleston Harbor and hear a scrape along the starboard side. I missed seeing the mooring buoy anchored about five yards off the dock, and a later inspection shows two deep scratches in the gelcoat close to the waterline. This is another good reminder to not become complacent and to be alert to not hit anything in these crowded waters.

We are past the NO WAKE zone, and boaters are motoring by as we approach the Isle of Palms Connector Bridge. It is decision time, for the original inland passage followed Hamlin Creek next to the island. Once across the inlet, it followed Conch Creek behind Sullivan's Island. Surveying the scene, the shore blanket of the wind and the adverse effect of the tide near Breach Inlet are factors for making the shortest, fastest sail. The end is within reach, but I dismiss the longer sail for the expedient course in order to not miss the incoming tide into Charleston Harbor. Crossing under the bridge, we head to the northern side of the ICW, staying away from the impairment of the wind from Little Goat Island. We in fact stay close to the marsh, where sections of rock do not impede our course.

Where Swinton Creek crosses the ICW, the opening to the south displays the first view to Breach Inlet. All along this route the direction of the current changes, depending on what side of the nearest inlet we are on. The low bridge crossing Breach Inlet between Isle of Palms and Sullivan's Island is visible, and the perspective from this distance is all white water from under the bridge to the inlet beach sand. Straight down the ICW is the Ben Sawyer Bridge, crossing over to Sullivan's Island from the mainland. It is a swing bridge, disabled in 1989 from the winds of Hurricane Hugo until one lane was reopened weeks later. I pause to consider the vertical clearance, with *Kingfisher* in mind. Reading the chart, I calculate that we can easily pass under the thirty-one-foot vertical clearance without lowering the upper boom. In approaching the bridge, we encounter the strongest adverse tide today. The incoming waters flow into the harbor from the ocean and pour into this waterway behind Sullivan's Island, known as Sullivans Narrows. With other boat traffic slowed due to NO WAKE signs, *Kingfisher* passes underneath this bridge for the first time. The rusted beams, the cars humming over the open road deck and the excess used grease oozing out of the mechanism fittings do not promote trust when passing below this aging structure.

Once past the bridge, we move sharply toward the marsh edge again to avoid as much current as possible. We pass Toler's Cove marina to starboard, noting a kayaker in this creek. There is a lot of boat traffic, but the NO WAKE is maintained through here. A creek cuts over to a larger waterway, Jeanette Creek, which appears to flow all the way to the Mount Pleasant mainland. And over the marsh is the structure we have seen for some time but now positioned on the other side of Mount Pleasant: the Cooper River Bridge towers. A bend appears at the end of Sullivans Narrows ahead, and the sharp turn should take us out into Charleston Harbor.

We continue to hug the marsh and are ready to cut the corner around this turn. Yet from astern comes the loud, insistent beat of someone wanting to be heard. It is a sleek black craft, pounding out rap music on its stereo system. And there is movement aboard, especially from a slim young woman wearing a bathing suit that stretches the meaning of that clothing type. The boaters are partying, screaming, squealing, dancing. This is a crowded waterway, between the end of Sullivan's Island and the derelict piers of the Pitt Street Bridge, and this craft is profiling as if it were a low rider cruising along a downtown roadway: making the scene and being seen. Close to port, we pass two young, shirtless males in a johnboat, and there is no hint of the wave from them as they head toward the black craft. These guys are like two deer in headlights, their eyes fixed on the cavorting woman ahead. The view toward Fort

Moultrie, the cathedral tower and the residences along the shore are lost in this little small craft drama.

Around the bend, I jibe off quickly, heading close to the marsh on the Pitt Street side to search for some peace away from the traffic. Inexplicably, the black craft is following my course, I'm sure looking for their way. It finally corrects and heads out into the harbor toward the shipping channel and the peninsula in the distance. Away from the beat, we sail toward the Mount Pleasant Channel along the edge of the shore and town. All of a sudden, we are out into this large and historical body of water, and in the continuing clear skies, there are magnificent sights: Fort Sumter, Castle Pinckney, the Charleston peninsula and watercraft everywhere. I experience the exhilarating feeling of many past mariners making this turn from the inland passage into the expanse of this majestic harbor and the passing into a man-made landscape of town and waterfront. We sail just outside of the docks of Mount Pleasant homes and farther on past the Old Village homes.

I change course from this channel out toward a shallow area a little offshore and can see vegetation sticking up from an exposed high spot. This patch of sand with some low vegetation is Crab Bank, and as we sail close by, the rookery comes alive. Pelicans nest in crowded conditions in this colony. Reflecting on my trips to Marsh Island in the center of Bulls Bay, it is amazing that these birds have chosen this spot in the midst of teeming civilization; surely there are better alternatives. And yet here they are, and the perimeter of the island is virtually clad with CLOSED AREA signs, I'm sure the work of DNR staff Felicia Sanders and Mark Spinks. Felicia has seen people running through the pelican nests playing Frisbee and has worked hard to educate the public about protecting these nesting colonies. Several kayaks are on the point as we sail pass, rounding up on a westerly course in the Hog Island Channel. Astern, the entrance to Shem Creek opens, and on the east side along Haddrell Point docks the shrimping fleet. Heading past a range marker, the current is still very strong in the last hour of incoming tide, and I am very happy that we have it in our favor.

In passing Hog Island, now known as Patriot's Point, the first container ship of the evening is outboard bound, pushing a nice bow wave. The evening cruiser *Pride of Charleston* is under sail and heading out toward Fort Johnson. We pass the point of the Patriot's Point marina. I imagine what it must have been like for Jonathan Lucas to organize the dismantling of the windmill on Hog Island and to transport the mechanical assembly, including the five-ton mill shaft, north to Mill Island.

Passing the marina, we sail in between the outer breakwater and the outermost dock. A group of young women approach the large catamaran to board for an evening cruise. Other people are busy with their large yachts. A few sailing craft also cruise across the harbor. The breakwater is covered with birds, populated with a large number of black skimmers. Ahead is the Cooper River Bridge, towering over these waters. Off to the west, in the bright haze of the lowering sun amidst the other urban structures, are the mast and spars of the *Spirit of South Carolina*, docked at the Charleston Maritime Center. This is the historical location of the wharf and home of Henry Laurens. From this town center, Laurens managed his widespread business interests, including his Wambaw Plantation off the South Santee River. His schooner, the *Wambaw*, plied these waters in transporting goods and supplies back and forth from the Santee plantation, and this schooner and his other smaller vessels surely traveled the inland passage.

Approaching the Cooper River Bridge, I take several photographs, framing the *Kingfisher*'s mast with the eastern tower. I do not take the center pass in the main shipping channel since another ship is also heading out to sea. We pass under this monumental structure, noticing a couple of walkers on the pedestrian lane far above. We sail on for the point ahead, where the Wando River branches off from the Cooper, and come up to closehauled for the public landing at Remley's Point. A Hobie 16 is landing near the ramp along the river's edge, and another Sunfish is battling the incoming tide to sail back. An unusual entrance to the landing is created by large metal and concrete pilings located every six feet parallel to the bank to regulate the boat traffic. Passing the last pile, we come around to the port tack and sail the final way in, dropping the sail and coasting to the floating dock, parallel to an active fishing dock on the other side of the three-section ramp. Stepping onto the dock, and tying up *Kingfisher*, mild leg muscle tension and aches are present despite all of my efforts to stretch intermittently throughout these twelve hours on the water. This is a busy ramp, and I drop the mast and secure *Kingfisher*. The last leg complete, I walk to land and make my phone call for the ride home.

The Inland Passage

Processing the trip takes some time. The next day, I figuratively pinch myself to make sure it was not a dream. One consequence is very real: the bay crossing took its toll in a very unusual way. The surfing of waves requires extensive shifting of weight fore and aft, sliding along the deck to catch waves and to avoid submarining. Taking a shower that Saturday night, the water stings my backside and I feel skin hanging loose on both sides. Further investigation reveals two silver dollar–sized blisters burned into my bottom during the bay crossing. Over a week later, these two areas are still tender and healing. A strong northeast wind comes back the following Sunday, but the recovery process keeps me onshore. I don't anticipate making this same sail again in my lifetime, but I expect I will be reminiscing and dreaming about the memorable passage for years to come.

BIBLIOGRAPHY

A number of primary and secondary sources were identified and used during the research for this book. The reader may wish to explore this information further by referring to the following sources.

Abedon, Emily P. "Lost and Found." *Charleston* (November 2006): 126–136.

Anderson, Christine. "Heroes of the Sea." *Georgetown Times,* July 24, 1999.

Bahr, Leonard N., and William P. Lanier. *The Ecology of Intertidal Oyster Reefs of the South Atlantic Coast: A Community Profile*. Washington, D.C.: U.S. Fish and Wildlife Service, Office of Biological Services, FWS/OBS-81/15, 1981.

Baldwin, William P. *Inland Passages: Making a Lowcountry Life*. Charleston, SC: The History Press, 2004.

Baldwin, William P., and John M. Lofton Jr. *The Loggerheads of Cape Romain*. McClellanville, SC: Cape Romain Migratory Bird Refuge, U.S. Biological Survey, 1940. Reprint, McClellanville, SC: Village Museum, 1999.

Barnwell, Robert Woodward Sr. *Dawn at Daufuskie and Other Poems*. N.p., 1936.

Bellis, Vincent J. *Ecology of Maritime Forests of the Southern Atlantic Coast: A Community Profile*. Washington, D.C.: U.S. Department of the Interior, National Biological Service, Biological Report 30, 1995.

Bishop, Nathaniel Holmes. *Voyage of the Paper Canoe*. Santa Barbara, CA: Narrative Press, 1878.

Brennessel, Barbara. *Diamonds in the Marsh: A Natural History of the Diamondback Terrapin*. Hanover, NH: University Press of New England, 2006.

Bridges, Anne Baker Leland, and Roy Williams III. *St. James Santee Plantation Parish: History and Records, 1685–1925*. Spartanburg, SC: Reprint Company, 1997.

Burrell, V.G., Jr. *Species Profiles: Life Histories and Environmental Requirements of Coastal Fishes and Invertebrates (South Atlantic)—American Oyster*. Washington, D.C.: U.S. Fish & Wildlife Service, Biologist Report 82(11.57), U.S. Army Corps of Engineers TR EL-82-4, 1986.

Cape Romain Lighthouses. National Register of Historic Places Inventory, Nomination Form.

"Capt. Wm. Leland Drowned." *Charleston News & Courier*, May 26, 1911.

Carney, Judith A. *Black Rice*. Cambridge, MA: Harvard University Press, 2001.

Castro, Jose I. "The Shark Nursery of Bulls Bay, South Carolina, with a Review of the Shark Nurseries of the Southeastern Coast of the United States." *Environmental Biology of Fishes* 38 (October 1993): 37–48.

Clary, Margie Willis. *The Beacons of South Carolina*. Orangeburg, S.C.: Sandlapper Publishing, 2005.

Dawsey, Sarah. Report on Management of Atlantic Loggerhead Sea Turtle Nests on Cape Romain National Wildlife Refuge. 2007.

Earley, Lawrence S. *Looking for Longleaf: The Fall and Rise of an American Forest*. Chapel Hill: University of North Carolina Press, 2004.

Edelson, S. Max. *Plantation Enterprise in Colonial South Carolina*. Cambridge, MA: Harvard University Press, 2006.

Fraser, Walter J., Jr. *Lowcountry Hurricanes: Three Centuries of Storms at Sea and Ashore*. Athens: University of Georgia Press, 2006.

Fulton, Robert. "Report on the Practicability of Navigating with Steam Boats, on the Southern Waters of the United States." New York: E. Conrad, 1813.

Hayes, Miles O., and Jacqueline Michel. *A Coast for all Seasons: A Naturalist's Guide to the Coast of South Carolina*. Columbia SC: Pandion Books, 2008.

Herman, Louis M. "Cognitive Characteristics of Dolphins." In *Cetacean Behavior: Mechanisms and Functions*. Edited by L.M. Herman. New York: John Wiley and Sons, 1980.

Hills, Richard. *Power from the Wind: A History of Windmill Technology*. New York: Cambridge University Press, 1994.

History of the Waterways of the Atlantic Coast of the United States. NWS 83-10, January 1983. http://usace.army.mil/publications/misc.nws83-10/toc.htm (accessed September 1, 2007).

Hopkins-Murphy, Sally R., and Joan S. Seithel. "Documenting the Value of Volunteer Effort for Sea Turtle Conservation in South Carolina." *Chelonian Conservation and Biology* 4, no. 4 (April 2005): 930–34.

Hurley, Suzanne, Cameron Linder and Marta Leslie Thacker. *Historical Atlas of the Rice Plantations of Georgetown County and the Santee River.* Columbia: South Carolina Department of Archives and History for the Historic Ricefields Association Inc., 2001.

Johnsgard, Paul A. *Cormorants, Darters, and Pelicans of the World.* Washington, D.C.: Smithsonian Institution Press, 1993.

Joyner, Charles. *Down by the Riverside: A South Carolina Slave Community.* Chicago: University of Illinois Press, 1984.

King, Richard J. "To Kill a Cormorant." *Natural History* (March 2009): 24–29.

King, Stewart R. "Family Refuses to Give up on Trawler Missing 11 Days." *Charleston Evening Post*, August 5, 1968.

Kracker, Laura M. *Literature Review for a Resource Characterization of Cape Romain National Wildlife Refuge.* NOAA Technical memorandum NOS-NCCOS-CCEHBR-0008, July 2003.

Laurens, Henry. *The Papers of Henry Laurens.* Vol. V. Edited by G.C. Rogers Jr. and D.R. Chesnutt. Columbia: University of South Carolina Press, 1976.

Lawson, John. *A New Voyage to Carolina.* Chapel Hill: University of North Carolina Press, 1967.

Lennon, Gered, Wiliam J. Neal, David M. Bush, Orrin H. Pilkey, Matthew Stutz and Jane Bullock. *Living with the South Carolina Coast.* Durham, NC: Duke University Press, 2002.

Lofton, Alexander Lucas. *The Lucases of Haddrells Point.* Book I, 1785–1835. N.p., 1999.

"A Lucas Memorandum." *South Carolina Historical Society Magazine* 69 (1968): 193.

Mackintosh, Margaret. "At Sixty, McClellanville Man Once More Cheats the Tide." In *Visible Village.* Edited by W.P. Baldwin. McClellanville, SC: McClellanville Arts Council, 1993.

Moore, Jamie W. *The Lowcountry Engineers: Military Missions and Economic Development in the Charleston District, U.S. Army Corps of Engineers.* Charleston, SC: District, 1982.

Peterson, Bo. "Humpback Beached on Cape Island." *Charleston Post and Courier*, January 13, 2006.

Pfaller, Josheph B., Colin J. Limpus and Karen A. Bjorndal. "Nest-site Selection in Individual Loggerhead Turtles and Consequences for Doomed-egg Relocation." *Conservation Biology* (August–October 2008): 239.

Pilkey, Orrin H., and Mary Edna Fraser. *A Celebration of the World's Barrier Islands*. New York: Columbia University Press, 2003.

"Plight of the Loggerhead Turtle." *New York Times*, September 27, 2007.

Popper, Arthur N. "Sound Emission and Detection by Delphinids." In *Cetacean Behavior: Mechanisms and Functions*. Edited by L.M. Herman. New York: John Wiley and Sons, 1980.

Porcher, Richard D., and Douglas A. Rayner. *A Guide to the Wildflowers of South Carolina*. Columbia: University of South Carolina Press, 2001.

Raynor, Bob. *Exploring Bull Island: Sailing and Walking Around a South Carolina Sea Island*. Charleston, SC: The History Press, 2005.

Robertson, David. *Denmark Vesey*. New York: Alfred A. Knopf, 1999.

Rogers, George C., Jr. *The History of Georgetown County, South Carolina*. Columbia: University of South Carolina Press, 1970.

Rutledge, Archibald. *Deep River: The Complete Poems of Archibald Rutledge*. Columbia, SC: R.L. Bryan, 1966.

Safina, Carl. *Voyage of the Turtle: In Pursuit of the Earth's Last Dinosaur*. New York: Henry Holt, 2007.

Sexton, Walter J. "The Post-Storm Hurricane Hugo Recovery of the Undeveloped Beaches Along the South Carolina Coast, 'Capers to the Santee Delta.'" *Journal of Coastal Research* 11, no. 4 (1995): 1020–25.

Sloan, Peggy E. "Residency Patterns, Seasonality and Habitat Use Among Bottlenose Dophins, *Tursiops Truncatus*, in the Cape Romain National Wildlife Refuge, SC." Master's thesis, University of North Carolina Wilmington, 2006.

Slocum, Joshua. *Sailing Alone Round the World and Voyage of the Liberdade*. Norwich, England: Adlard Coles Limited, 1948.

Spence, E. Lee. *Shipwrecks, Pirates & Privateers: Sunken Treasures of the Upper South Carolina Coast, 1521–1865*. Charleston, SC: Narwhal Press, 1995.

———. *Shipwrecks of South Carolina and Georgia*. Sullivan's Island, SC: Sea Research Society, 1984.

Stokhuyzen, Frederick. *The Dutch Windmill*. Bussum, Holland: Van Dishoeck, 1973.

Tibbetts, John H. "The Bird Chase." *Coastal Heritage* 15, no. 4 (Spring 2002): 3–13.

Whitaker, J. David, John W. McCord, Philip P. Maier, Albert L. Segars, Megan L. Rekow, Norm Shea, Jason Ayers and Rocky Browder. *An Ecological Characterization of Coastal Hammock Islands in South Carolina.* Charleston: Marine Resources Division, South Carolina Department of Natural Resources, 2004.

Wiegert, Richard G., and Byron J. Freeman. *Tidal Salt Marshes of the Southeast Atlantic Coast: A Community Profile.* Washington, D.C.: U.S. Department of the Interior, Fish and Wildlife Service, Biological Report 85(7.29), 1990.

MAPS, CHARTS AND PLATS

Bowman, John. *Plan for 16,992 Acres on Sixteen Islands on Bulls Bay and the Racoon Keys, Charleston District.* Surveyed by James Cross. Columbia: South Carolina Department of Archives & History, 1791.

Cape Romain Light Station, SC. Surveyed by H. Bamber. McClellanville, SC: Village Museum, 1893.

Casino Creek to Beaufort River, Intracoastal Waterway, South Carolina. Washington, D.C.: NOAA, 1991.

Lynch, Thomas. *Plan for 5,560 Acres on Big and Little Racoon Keys, Charleston District.* Surveyed by James Cross. Columbia: South Carolina Department of Archives & History, 1788.

Preliminary Chart of Bull's Bay, SC. United States Coast Survey, 1859. South Carolina Historical Society, Charleston.

Preliminary Sketch of Winyah Bay & Cape Romain Shoals, SC. United States Coast Survey, 1854. South Carolina Historical Society, Charleston.

Winyah Bay Entrance to Isle of Palms, South Carolina. Washington, D.C.: NOAA, 1980.

INDEX

ABOUT THE AUTHOR

Courtesy of Susan Raynor.

B ob Raynor is a longtime resident of Awendaw, South Carolina, a community bordering on the magnificent Cape Romain National Wildlife Refuge. Bob continues to work as a recreation therapist in MUSC's Institute of Psychiatry and Center for Drug and Alcohol Programs. His passions for sailing, the natural world and history came together for his first book, *Exploring Bull Island: Sailing and Walking Around a South Carolina Sea Island,* and continue to motivate his ongoing explorations. Bob devotes time to service work for the U.S. Fish and Wildlife Service and other efforts to protect this section of the coast.

YOU MIGHT
ALSO ENJOY

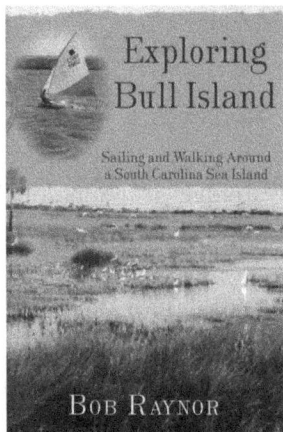

Exploring Bull Island
Sailing and Walking Around a South Carolina Sea Island
Bob Raynor
978.1.59629.010.5 • 6 x 9 • 192 pp. • $19.99

During Raynor's monthly trips—by sailing and walking around the island—the natural and cultrual history of this Sea Island is revealed.

9 7 8 1 5 4 0 2 3 4 6 9 8